MODERN SPIRITUALITY

MODERN SPIRITUALITY

A GUIDE TO THE HEART OF MINDFULNESS, MEDITATION, AND THE ART OF HEALING

Benjamin W. Decker

ROCKRIDGE
PRESS

Interior and Cover Designer: Jami Spittler
Art Producer: Samantha Ulban
Editor: Lia Ottaviano
Production Editor: Matthew Burnett

Photography © Leblanc Catherine/Alamy, p.116.
All images used under license © Shutterstock and iStock.
Author photograph courtesy of Ali Wolfe.

ISBN: Print 978-1-64739-815-6 | eBook 978-1-64739-490-5

R0

TO ALL OF MY BROTHERS, SISTERS,
AND COUSINS, THEIR FAMILIES, THEIR CHILDREN,
AND THEIR CHILDREN'S CHILDREN.

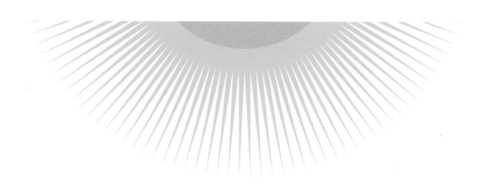

CONTENTS

INTRODUCTION: MODERN SPIRITUALITY FOR EVERYONE

We live in a time when ancient prophecies are finally being fulfilled. Every surviving faith tradition has one story or another of its great teachers and prophets gazing into the future and seeing a day when all people around the world—from all cultures, tribes, and traditions would come together in the spirit of peace. Today is that day.

As the world becomes smaller and smaller through technological advances, humans are realizing how similar they really are. That similarity includes our faith. We have found that, more often than not, when it comes down to it, each faith tradition centers on nearly identical core principles of unity, compassion, personal responsibility, forgiveness, eternity, and infinite possibilities—or *miracles*.

People of every nation, tribe, and language have awakened to the realization we are really one people, living on a very small planet in a very large universe. Spiritual evolution is taking place—not through renunciation of our old faith traditions, but through a metaphysical reconciliation. It is not that God or the universe has changed. *We have.*

Modern Spirituality is a guide to understanding and navigating this change. It is intended to be a completely new, practical expression of the universal spiritual concepts found in all major world faith traditions. Presented through the lens of modern psychological and scientific understanding, *Modern Spirituality* addresses the most pressing spiritual challenges of our generation and provides proven techniques to equip us to lead more meaningful, fulfilling lives by tuning in to our *higher natures*.

The *lower nature* is our physical nature, which was born and will one day die. The lower nature, sometimes called "the natural man" or the "animal nature," responds to materialistic urges and automatic biological cravings. The *higher nature* is our spiritual, or divine, nature, which was never born and will never die and operates on an almost completely opposite set of characteristics from our lower nature. Whereas those who continue to operate from the default lower nature are held back from spiritual evolution by their free will and circumstances, those who engage with the wisdom of higher nature experience a spiritual rebirth and become purified, more advanced, more powerful, and more peaceful.

Spiritual faith traditions have collected extraordinary wisdom over the ages about how to discipline our lower nature—techniques that allow us to renounce its characteristics and cultivate inner awareness of our higher nature.

The goal of this book is to draw from those traditions and beyond to help you access your higher nature. In doing so, it will help you find your purpose, provide spiritual support for any difficulty or hardship you may encounter, and empower and enable you to heal. This book is a gift for anyone called to spirituality and who feels connected to that global sense of spirituality. Anyone at any phase of their spiritual process and from any religious background (or no religious background) can learn and benefit from the journey presented here.

Modern Spirituality assumes seven core principles, drawn from an analysis of all major world traditions, which will be explored and applied through different topics and exercises. These core principles are:

1. You are a child of God, the creative source of the universe, born into a world designed for your growth, learning, and happiness.

2. Body, mind, spirit, society, and nature are inextricably linked.

3. You are extremely powerful and all your power is accessible only in the present moment.

4. The mind and spirit operate according to metaphysical laws, which can be learned and applied.

5. The body and emotions operate according to physical laws, which can be learned and applied.

6. Humanity has a dual nature: physical, considered the "lower nature," and spiritual, considered the "higher nature."

7. The path of spiritual development is the ongoing study and intentional applied practice of these things through a threefold approach of application of spiritual principles, personal spiritual exercise, and community spiritual exercise.

This book is intended to be a practical guide, not a theological treatise. In the context of this book, all of these words and concepts—*God*, your *heart*, your *soul*, the *universe*, your *higher self*—are generally different ways of referring to the same infinite higher power. I invite you to engage with whatever word or concept you need to tap into your spiritual nature and to be flexible, as I use them relatively interchangeably.

This book is divided into 11 chapters, each intended to build on the last and to take the reader through a complete spiritual healing journey from beginning to end while creating the context for an ongoing spiritual practice. Each chapter breaks down a single concept to provide foundational context and ends with an exercise to allow you to put into play the ideas, skills, and approach you've just learned. Exercises include meditations, mind-body exercises, journal prompts, and other tools drawn from the best resources available today.

I began my own spiritual journey growing up as a member of The Church of Jesus Christ of Latter-day Saints. At a young age, I was presented with great teachings that conditioned me to be open to the idea that spiritual understanding can evolve. A core tenet of my family's tradition is the continuity of revelation—the idea that each generation would receive its own prophetic guidance specific to its needs, circumstances, and level of consciousness. I learned about prayer, personal study, meditation, and seeking truth anywhere it may be found—principles that have a place in one form or another in the heart of every spiritual tradition.

Though I entered the priesthood as a teenager, I spent my 20s immersing myself in a study I affectionately called "collaborative religion." I explored Hindu and Buddhist monasteries, numerous Christian denominations, practiced Tai Chi and took Mindfulness Trainings. I attended lectures at the Theosophical Society, the University of Philosophical Research, and the Carl Jung Institute. I participated in esoteric distance-learning programs and personal study programs based on universal spiritual themes with the goal of healing from trauma, overcoming character defects, "taming my lower nature," and demonstrating spirituality as a way of life. I became a meditation teacher, yoga instructor, energy work practitioner, and, eventually, opened a religiously pluralistic spiritual center in Venice Beach, California. I absorbed the esoteric teachings of many of the world's religions, always with an eye to their similarities rather than their differences.

In all the great traditions, the highest journey is the one we take to become more loving, more pure, and more whole. In Buddhism, it is called the Way of the Bodhisattva, and the first initiation on this path is activated by a moment of sincere compassion in one's heart. I invite you to open your heart and your mind to this reality: As you heal and grow spiritually, you offer great benefits to the world around you and to everyone with whom you come in contact. Society thirsts desperately for more spiritually awakened people to participate boldly and wisely in the economy, in enterprise, in governance, and in other spheres of influence.

My goal is not to convert or change you in any way, but to love you, accept you, support you, and walk hand in hand with you along this journey to a more beautiful world.

Let's begin.

Only You Can Write Your Story

IMAGINE THERE ARE TWO PATHS before you: the one you are on and one that veers to the right. The path you are on is wide and seems to meander comfortably. It's a little easier to stay on and, from what you can tell right now, it has some beautiful plants growing along it and will likely take you to some lovely views. The path to the right seems to be a bit more challenging. Perhaps it's a little steeper or a bit narrower, so it requires more ongoing, consistent effort to walk it. But it also offers greater beauty; it's lined with gorgeous, exotic flowers, and if you keep following it, it will eventually lead to breath-taking views.

But each path doesn't just offer beauty. They both cross treacherous territory. Though the path you are on currently is easier to navigate, it has hidden perils that may catch you off guard. The path to the right has hidden perils, too. But if you take that path, it will prepare you intentionally, gradually, for those perils so, when they arise, you'll be ready.

Both paths provide the necessary opportunities for growth, and both lead to greater understanding and learning. But the path you are on represents the path of learning through unexpected obstacles and pain. The path to the right symbolizes making a life-changing commitment to dedication, study, and applied practice.

In Kabbalah, the ancient Jewish mystical tradition, the idea of the two paths is simplified by saying: You can choose to learn through the path of pain or through the path of joy. This does not mean there will be no joy on the path of pain or that there will be no pain on the spiritual path of joy. However, it does mean that a life of conscious dedication to spiritual development will equip you with the tools and skills to more masterfully and joyfully navigate challenges that do arise.

In our lives, these two paths are separated by one thing—your thoughts, beliefs, and the other things that make up your *inner narrative*. That's it. Joy and pain exist within the realm of our own perception.

In this first chapter, we will explore the inner narrative that unconsciously colors your life experiences. You will learn the basics of how to identify your automatic narrative path and how to work with your creative imagination to reframe the story. You'll also learn how to live consciously—a practice that will help you direct and connect yourself to your higher nature as you walk along the path.

The Stories We Tell About Ourselves

Each day we are faced with countless decisions. Some decisions—such as whether to get out of bed right now, what to eat for breakfast, or what we will do to prepare for the day—are small. Other decisions—such as where to work, what to study, and who to spend our time with—feel bigger. Every time we have a decision to make, we see all possible outcomes through the lens of our inner narrative, constructed by our inner dialogue.

Each of us has an ongoing reel of inner dialogue running 24/7 in our minds. It is made up of the thousands of different voices we've heard throughout our lives. Phrases and ideas that have been expressed to us or about us echo and morph in our minds, mixing and overlapping with our direct experiences and the internalized beliefs that come from them. "I got my sugar addiction from my parents" is an example of a story that can reinforce an unhealthy habit and belief about ourselves. Another could be, "I always make that mistake." Imagine all the different things anyone has ever said to you. Close your eyes for a moment and take a deep breath. What thoughts, words, and images come to mind? What story are you telling yourself?

If we are fortunate enough to be surrounded by wise, loving, positive people who support and encourage us, we are more likely to have an inner dialogue that allows us to experience confidence and strength, which leads to more powerful decision-making, often yielding more favorable results. If we find ourselves surrounded by people, circumstances, and content that overtly or unconsciously tear us down, the result is weakened decision-making, yielding unfavorable results.

But even if we've had experiences that led us to develop a negative inner narrative, change is possible. One of the most powerful tools for changing your inner narrative is meditation. Meditation gives you the ability to release the automatic behavioral patterns unconsciously informed by your inner narrative.

In compassion-based mindfulness meditation, we direct our awareness to the present moment, compassionately observing it exactly as it is, without any judgment or criticism. Breathing in and out, you signal to the body that it is in a safe place and time: right here, right now. This sense of safety sets in, gradually allowing the body to soften and relax. As the body relaxes, the subtle energy required to hold unconscious tension in the muscles and nervous system becomes available and that energy moves naturally where it is needed most. Your mind has more energetic resources to draw upon, to self-reflect and self-direct. You then "listen to yourself," meaning you listen to your thoughts with your inner ear, observe your thoughts with your inner eye, and observe your inner narrative—always maintaining an energetic field of compassion and nonjudgment.

As you begin to observe your inner narrative objectively and honestly, without judgment or shame, you begin to understand the ways your life is affected and informed by it. This recognition is one of the first steps that will move you off the default path of learning through pain and onto the conscious path of intentional spiritual development, learning through joy.

YOUR STORY AND YOUR BRAIN

Neuroplasticity is a term that refers to the brain's ability to change old synaptic connections and create new ones, based on learning and experiences—in short, it's how your brain develops its wiring. Because of neuroplasticity, the stories we tell ourselves repeatedly become engrained in our minds as fact. But just because our brain perceives a story as fact right now, doesn't mean change is impossible. Just as we have the ability to dig canals to redirect rivers to new destinations, we have the ability to establish new neural pathways, to rewrite these stories, establishing a new mind and new perspective altogether.

Explore Core Beliefs

Our longest-held and most deeply engrained perspectives exist in such an inner layer of ourselves that we identify with them; we believe we are them. These are our *core beliefs*.

When you were born into this world, there was a perfect light inside you that radiated through the perfect innocence of your infant body, just like every other living being. Life experiences, traumas, and our longest-held inner narratives act as templates and filters, changing that light. Think of it this way: A red lightbulb and a blue lightbulb have the same pure light radiating from them and were made in the same factory with the same materials. But, at some point, different elements were added to make them emit different colors. The nature of the light did not change—only the outer expression of the light.

We are these lightbulbs. Everything you have experienced has left an unconscious imprint on your psyche—it changed the color of your light.

Our work is to recognize that we are made up of causes and effects, to make the unconscious conscious. Then, we must consciously override this default programming to reclaim our pure light.

One powerful way to disengage from the negative associations that have distorted your worldview is reconciliation with your core beliefs. Our core beliefs act as the larger framework through which we experience everything in our lives. Core beliefs govern how we live and yet, they are rarely obvious to us at first. They're also rarely 100-percent true, even if they feel or seem that way.

There are major problems in the world today that can be solved when we reconcile with our core beliefs and learn to rewrite the way we see the world. Things such as racism, sexism, and other forms of prejudice are based on unconscious programming from the world around us. To reconcile means to make peace. Accept those core beliefs. Some of them may not resonate with your real conscious understanding of the world.

To reconcile your core beliefs, you must first recognize them. Start by seeing yourself fearlessly and objectively. With an open heart and mind, try to observe your personality, your emotional patterns, and the way you show up in relationships.

Once you've spent time observing your core beliefs, it's time to write about them. Mindful writing practices and regular journaling provide the opportunity to observe and work with your contextual core beliefs. When we write something down, we reflect a bit more on how we'd like to express ourselves than when we just talk or think.

Try writing about how you feel. Describe your experiences, the challenges you face, and anything you find important. As you write, make an effort to write as honestly as possible to provide the clearest expression of where you are in the present moment. Then, read it back to yourself, aloud if possible. What is the overall attitudinal tone? Are there any negative or untrue beliefs that jump out?

RELEASE WHAT DOESN'T SERVE YOU

Growing up, I believed a lie: that I was not athletic. I decided at a young age that I was an intellectual and that sports and fitness were not in my wheelhouse and, therefore, not my top priority. This became a core belief. I was able to trace that belief back to a long list of childhood experiences: when I wasn't the fastest runner in gym class, when my older brothers left me in the dust on bike rides, or when my young, unskilled body could barely perform the exercises asked of it in karate, yoga, and gymnastics classes.

Once I was older and trying to release my unsupportive core beliefs, I found my core belief that I was "not athletic" was actually a core belief that I was "not good enough" in a more general sense, and that I should keep to myself to avoid failure and embarrassment. I believed the superconfidence of professional athletes, billionaire entrepreneurs, genius scientists, and respected church leaders that I saw projected onto the world and I internalized the belief that they were fundamentally of a better nature than I was.

This kind of distorted belief is all too common and does not serve one's path of highest growth and fulfillment. This isn't to say you shouldn't look up to anyone; there can be great power in looking to archetypal perfection for inspiration. But it's also important to accept the uniqueness of your individual life path, recognize where you are now, and realize you are always changing and growing. You are in a constant process of unfolding. Allow greatness in others to inspire and motivate you, but don't let it discourage and intimidate you. Seek to create, not to compete.

Releasing unsupportive core beliefs is also important for another reason: When we let go of limiting beliefs that no longer serve us, we make room for the next lesson to learn. Nature works a bit at a time. Think of a snake shedding its old skin or a tree as it grows gradually each year. Imagine your spiritual maturation in this same way. You will learn a little bit at a time. You will shed one layer at a time.

LET IT GO

The sooner we can release what doesn't serve us, the sooner we can make room for the things that truly matter. There are numerous ways to release a belief, but here are the four fundamental steps:

1. Identify the belief that does not serve you and all the ways it shows up in your life.

2. Recognize its possible sources, letting go of any shame or judgment associated with it.

3. Powerfully decide to let it go.

4. Commit to new ways of thinking and operating.

CREATE SUPPORTIVE STORIES

You don't need to experience a sudden or major life change to begin reframing your personal narrative. You can start right now, by cultivating a new attitude—that of the positive onlooker. This means taking a breath and creating a certain degree of detachment from what you're experiencing in the moment— the emotions you're having, the thoughts going through your head, and the circumstances that surround you—and trying to interpret them with hope and positivity. When we see our own circumstances through a positive lens, we begin to see possibilities, whereas a negative attitude only highlights problems.

If you're not sure whether you have a positive or negative attitude, look around you. What do you see? Do you see problems and disorder? Or, do you see blessings and abundance? Observe your mind. What kinds of thoughts come up? Do complaints and worries arise constantly? Or, do thoughts of hope and gratitude present themselves?

Imagine that every single word you think or speak sends invisible ripples into the world, in all directions around you, creating subtle changes in the universe. Imagine that a thought as simple as "I am grateful" could send out a message to the world around you, causing more of that which you are grateful for to present itself. This idea is the basis of the Law of Attraction and Repulsion.

The Law of Attraction and Repulsion is the metaphysical law that explains how and why we find ourselves in the circumstances that surround us. It describes that we magnetically attract *that which we are*—that like attracts like—and that we repel that which we are unlike. This means the thoughts we think, the energy we hold, and the words we say create our experience and inform our relationship to our circumstances, which then create the kinds of decisions we make in the midst of those circumstances.

By creating supportive stories for ourselves, we begin attracting more positive things into our world. Rather than allowing ourselves to move through life at the "effect" of our circumstances, we can co-create our experience by taking responsibility for how we respond to what life gives us. Your mind automatically attempts to answer questions. If you find that your mental narrative has become negative, ask yourself, "How can I see this situation differently?"

Imagine you're in a situation where you're learning something new. Notice the story running in your mind. Instead of telling yourself, "I've always had a hard time remembering details," reframe it into a story that creates a more supportive inner atmosphere. Tell yourself something like, "This is all very new to me but I can learn new things. I can pay attention and learn to get the hang of this." We don't want to cross the line into telling ourselves flat-out lies, so this definitely carries a disclaimer: You have to learn your own nuance. But get out of the self-judging, self-cursing zone and talk to yourself as you would someone you love—with encouragement and kindness.

A practice of daily review journaling can be a potent tool for changing your perspective. Daily review journaling is done at the end of the day before going to bed. Take time to reflect on the day and write about it. Tell the story of the day, especially the good and positive experiences, with generous detail. As you write about the challenges of the day, reflect on the question, "How can I see this situation differently?" As you ask yourself this question, your mind will automatically provide responses to the different ways you can see the situation. Feel them and explain the challenges and problems of the day through the attitude of the positive onlooker.

USE YOUR STORY TO SPUR GROWTH

When we hear the word "initiation," we might think of activities performed by secret societies, religious institutions, or social organizations to test and initiate new members to determine whether they have really become "one of them." But life itself carries a natural initiatory process. An initiation is just an activation, a test of all you have learned and cultivated. The death of a loved one is an initiation. Being struck by lightning or bitten by a snake are initiations. Getting your first job, losing a job, beginning or ending a relationship—these are all initiations.

In Indigenous traditions, the spiritual development journey is linked with nature and natural experiences. Someone who goes through a difficult or painful experience and emerges on the other side psychologically intact is revered for their wisdom and power, having gained spiritual authority because of the experience. These experiences are referred to as "shamanic initiations." Sometimes, these rites of passage are intentionally created, like a plant medicine journey or a vision quest.

To walk through the gates of initiation is to enter a new season of life, where new understanding is gained. These challenging experiences become raw power for us to draw upon and work with. Through the eyes of an initiate, failure becomes a learning opportunity.

All your mental and physical energy must be focused on the present moment's circumstances, exactly as they are. Not as they once were, not as you wish they'd be, not as you're afraid they'll become, but exactly as they are *now*.

The present moment, however, is not a dot on a timeline. It is a living, moving, dynamic experience made up of the past, building and creating the future. Learn to reframe past experiences so you can harness them to drive yourself into a fulfilling future. The only way to do this is to start right now and to practice mental reframing consistently. Practice observing the present moment and your automatic reactions and impulses to it. Breathe through them and reframe the automatic narrative that arrives through the lens of the positive onlooker. This takes practice, but eventually, you can make it a habit.

The exercise for this chapter will help you ask relevant questions, listen to your mind's responses, and begin to establish a new relationship with your inner narrative. This will help you recalibrate to deeper, truer core beliefs and establish a firm foundation upon which you may build your spiritual practice.

MANTRA MAGIC

The word "mantra" commonly refers to a phrase or sound repeated silently or aloud in the course of meditation. When the mantra is in an ancient language, like Latin or Sanskrit, it engages the brain's plasticity, making it more flexible and open to suggestion. Ancient languages are said to have been formed from a deeper level of consciousness with multidimensional applications, as opposed to modern language, which serves a more utilitarian purpose. For this reason, I include relevant Latin mantras (as well as their meaning) throughout this book.

RESTORING THE FOUNDATION

The following exercise is designed to help you effect positive change within your life.

TIME 30 TO 60 MINUTES

WHAT YOU'LL NEED

- ▶ Journal and pen (for any exercises, a laptop, a phone with a notepad app, or a few blank sheets of lined paper will work, too, but I recommend keeping a dedicated journal)
- ▶ Comfortable place to sit where you won't be interrupted
- ▶ Timer

OPTIONAL

You may choose to make this exercise more ceremonially significant by playing meditative or sacred music, lighting a few white candles, wearing all white, anointing yourself with essential oils such as frankincense or lavender, keeping a mirror nearby (for step 5), or taking a purifying shower or bath before you begin.

GET STARTED

1. Ask yourself the following key questions and fearlessly write out the answers in your journal. Write exactly what comes to mind, even if it is negative or seems unremarkable. The goal of this first step is to identify the state of your current narrative.

- ➤ **Past:** Where am I from? Who are my parents? Why was I born?

- ➤ **Present:** Where am I? Why am I the way I am? What are the factors or circumstances that most influence my life right now?

- ➤ **Future:** Where am I going? What is my purpose? Who am I becoming?

2. Take a few minutes to meditate silently.

   - ➤ As you meditate, breathe into your heart center, allowing every inhale to strengthen your love, compassion, and acceptance.

   - ➤ Throughout your meditation, allow your exhales to bring a wave of relaxation through every part of your body, calming the lower nature and releasing any tension.

   - ➤ With every exhale, silently repeat the mantra *tabula rasa*, which means "clean slate."

   - ➤ Visualize white light moving through every part of your brain, nervous system, and body, wiping away old stories, unhealthy habits, and unsupportive narratives.

3. Turn to a new page in your journal and ask yourself the same questions from step 1, but this time, imbue your answers with the following universal truths as well as the attitude of the positive onlooker:

➤

- ▶ **Past:** I am a child of the creator of the universe, born into a world designed for my growth, learning, and happiness.

- ▶ **Present:** I am exactly where I am supposed to be for my learning and development.

- ▶ **Future:** I am part of a great divine plan, perfectly orchestrated for my spiritual and physical evolutionary development.

4. Take a few more minutes to meditate as you did in step 2.

  - ▶ With every exhale, silently repeat the mantra *terra firma,* which means "solid ground."

  - ▶ Visualize white light moving through every part of your brain, nervous system, and body, anchoring in place this new narrative. Imagine that light reaching down into the ground beneath you like the roots of a tree, stabilizing and grounding you.

5. Finally, recite what you have written from step 3 with enthusiasm, joy, and energy activating your entire body. You may choose to look in a mirror as you do this, or record it to listen to later.

6. When you finish, stand up and stretch your body in any way that feels comfortable for you, sending a signal to the mind and body that something new is settling in.

7. Go about your day, allowing yourself to be a little more present than usual, making a special effort to make small changes that support a positive inner narrative.

WRAP UP

In your journal, describe the exercise, the different elements you added, the time of day you practiced, and anything you felt throughout the process. Describe any visions or insight you had so you can deepen your connection to this and reflect on it later. As you age, you will be grateful you kept records of your meaningful spiritual experiences and initiations.

GO DEEPER

Research shows it can take anywhere from 21 to 66 days to form a habit. This exercise will be most powerful if you continue with steps 4 through 7 on a daily basis for three weeks or longer.

Rewire and Reconnect

ABOUT 10 YEARS AFTER HIGH school graduation, I ran into a former friend. I have to admit, I couldn't remember her name and barely recognized her face. But she remembered me. In fact, she recalled an elaborate story about an experience we shared as teens. At first, I thought she mistook me for someone else! But, after a while, I started to remember the experience. I had let go of those memories and moved on from them, because for me, there was pain and embarrassment associated with them. For her, it was a juicy scandal that kept high school interesting. For me, it was a psychological and social roadblock I worked hard to overcome and move beyond. I had actually gone to therapy to process and heal from the experience she recalled so nonchalantly.

If it hadn't been for that painful, embarrassing high school experience, I likely would not have been pushed to explore therapy and mindfulness, both of which accelerated my psychological and spiritual maturation. But on that day, I barely remembered the experience in my conscious mind because, through hard work and consistent effort, my brain had rewired itself and had established new behavioral patterns. I had grown up, reconnected with my higher nature, and overcome the drama of the experience. It wasn't exactly suppressed in my memory, but my new life and new way of being had taken hold, creating new neural networks in my brain, and frankly, I became a better version of myself because of it. I was living a new normal.

Do you remember learning how to walk, talk, or read? Nature has a way of "letting go" of certain memories that don't seem relevant anymore. When we make a major change in our lives, we often forget what life was like before that change took place. It's not that our memory becomes erased; it's just that we have a completely new life experience now and the brain doesn't regularly remind itself of old ways of seeing and doing things. We don't want to suppress our past experiences, but we do want to move beyond them.

The global faith traditions describe this as rebirth. When we experience a spiritual rebirth, part of us dies and new innocence is born. In neuroscience, we can liken this "rebirth" to what happens when a new neural network is established due to a meaningful experience. This chapter is intended to support you in invoking and recognizing meaningful experiences to help rewire your brain and nervous system. This will help you evolve and overcome any negative patterns that may be preventing happiness, fulfillment, and a more pure expression of your divine nature and life's purpose.

LIFE ON AUTOPILOT

The majority of the body's actions are taken automatically. In fact, many of the body's functions happen without our awareness of them, like the release of certain hormones, the function of the liver, the gallbladder, digestion, and so on.

The same is true about the mind. Habits are established naturally as a way of doing things a little more efficiently. If a behavior is repeated numerous times, each repetition affirms its importance and relevance to the nervous system, and the brain and body begin working unconsciously to make the process more efficient for next time.

Habits are neutral, as far as the mind is concerned. But to our higher nature, some habits are wise and other habits are unwise.

The great news is, through the applied principle of neural plasticity, your brain and body are designed to do as you tell them. So, we have the ability to interrupt the pattern of unwise habits and activate the formation of new ones.

First, we need to learn the basics of how habitual behavior works. Habits, even bad ones, begin innocently enough as a first-time experience. That experience imprints the body and mind with data about circumstances, the environment, sensory input (like thoughts, sights, or smells), and any reward associated with it. Intentional habits are generated through a practice of rituals and routines, where we work consciously with the habit-forming process to lay the groundwork for a new healthy or desirable habit to take hold.

THE ANATOMY OF A HABIT

Here are the four major components of a habit:

1. **SIGNAL:** A trigger, signal, or cue is activated, sending a message to the brain: "When *this* happens, it's time to do *that*." When your alarm goes off in the morning, it's a signal that it's time to get up and out of bed. There are three main kinds of signals: environmental (locations, buildings, sounds, smells), social (family, friends, certain groups, individuals, or communities), and emotional (stress, anxiety, excitement, anger, loneliness, exhaustion, depression, worry).

2. **DESIRE:** The brain receives the signal and seeks to provide the necessary means to navigate it. The more intense the signal, the more intense the desire. For example, if you have childhood trauma relating to personal insecurity and the need for validation, hearing that someone you feel competitive with has received accolades could trigger the desire to bad-mouth them, or harm their success. It could also trigger the desire to withdraw, numb, overeat, etc.

3. **RESPONSE:** After the desire is activated, a rapid-fire process occurs and the brain tells the body exactly what to do next. It will draw upon past experiences to figure out which action will provide the best reward. These actions come in three main forms: behavioral (routine, ritual, action), emotional (anxiety, irritability, anger), and chemical (alcohol, caffeine, drugs, other substances).

4. **REINFORCEMENT:** Once the response is acted upon, the brain releases dopamine as a reward. This acts as a natural affirmation of the response to the signal and reinforces it for future circumstances where the signal may take place. The next time you receive that signal, you are likely to respond the same way.

Everyone is different and every person's triggers are unique. Each person's response to their triggers is also highly individualized.

KNOW THY TRIGGERS

1. Reflect on your top three unhealthy habits, like smoking, numbing out with TV or social media, etc.

2. Observe when the craving to engage those unhealthy habits arises and journal about the triggers, signals, or cues that cause you to crave the unhealthy behavior.

3. Avoid your triggers when possible.

4. Create a strategy for interrupting the response to those triggers by introducing a new behavior to take the place of the old habit, like taking a yoga class, meditating, learning a new language, or even just drinking a tall glass of water.

How Our Habits Shape Us

When we repeat an action or behavior, we tell our body and brain that the behavior is in alignment with our intentions and goals. If we continue a daily ritual, the brain and body will continue to follow that ritual, as if you have asked it to do so. If we practice something one time, that is the one opportunity for the neurons to fire in that specific way. If we practice something regularly over time, that neural firing becomes neural *wiring*, and a more efficient pathway is developed forming a new habit.

In the Buddhist tradition, *samsara* refers to the cycle of repeating old lessons. Often, this is in reference to past lives, but as one ancient aphorism says, "Every day is a new life to a wise person." Liberation from samsara is the experience of total freedom, breaking loose from the chains that hold us down.

Habits can have positive power. All of the world's faith traditions ask their followers to infuse daily life with spiritual rituals like daily prayer, meditation, scripture study, and the blessing of food to take gradual steps toward spiritual enlightenment and exaltation. The word "ritual" comes from the same etymological sources as the words "rite" and "right," implying that a ritual is doing something *right*; doing something *correctly*. As we practice infusing our lives with rituals, if we do them intentionally through applied neuroscience, we can begin to make them our habits.

Ask any fitness instructor, medical doctor, or nutritionist: Although taking healthy actions once in a blue moon may be technically better than never taking them at all, the real power is in developing healthy habits. Healthy habits create a healthy lifestyle, whereas unhealthy habits create an unhealthy lifestyle. A bodybuilder did not become a bodybuilder by waking up and going to the gym only once. It takes years of consistency and dedication to the task. Advanced spiritual students did not wake up one day enlightened. The Buddha had to practice serious discipline and study for *decades* before his infamous moment of enlightenment under the Bodhi tree. Jesus Christ was raised in a community that prioritized spiritual ordinances, and he had to train, practice, and study for years before his miracle-working ministry began.

Everything we do, see, eat, drink, hear, study, believe, and experience contributes to our internal makeup and the data that our unconscious mind works with to create our behaviors and thought patterns.

HABIT VERSUS ADDICTION

Sometimes, we casually use the words "habit" and "addiction" to describe the same behavior. But the truth is there is a substantial difference between a behavior that is considered habitual and one considered addictive. Three factors constitute the primary difference between a habit and an addiction, all related to response to triggers.

1. The reliability of a dopamine release from a substance or behavior.

2. The speed of the dopamine release.

3. The intensity of the dopamine release.

In cases where the reliability, speed, and intensity of the dopamine release are all "high," the possibility of addiction increases.

PREPARE TO TRANSFORM

You will find that going on a spiritual journey is not always easy. The inertia of your old way of living can make it challenging to move beyond your past. But remember, in every spiritual tradition, there is a necessary initiatory process. In that process, the initiate is trained and taught in the ways of the new path. Preparation is a necessary part of the process. From a metaphysical perspective, preparing for something is a crucial part of actually doing it!

In preparing for a physical journey, you need to anticipate the environment, the terrain, and any potential obstacles along the way. The same is true on the spiritual journey—but because the work being done is internal, the obstacles lie within. The only way to begin to recognize the obstacles that may arise is through developing a self-reflective practice.

The ancient Greek aphorism, "Know thyself," was said to have been written in the courtyard of the temple of Apollo, the god of light and war. This implies that going to battle must require the light of wisdom and that the wisdom required must be the knowledge of one's self. The spiritual initiate must recognize their own triggers and unhealthy behaviors, then interrupt the process, instill new, healthier behavioral responses, and make them into habits.

Preparing means looking to the future and providing for yourself in advance, anticipating future needs, and setting yourself up for success. Not only do we need to set ourselves up for success, we need to *establish the habit* of setting ourselves up for success.

The greatest benefit of rewiring to reconnect is that you have the support of automatic patterns in the brain and body. The body and brain become your greatest allies. This process can also help us get to know ourselves better, achieve more clarity on what we really want, tap into our true selves, achieve our higher purpose, and be our best for ourselves and others. The true spiritual path is not just about understanding and applying spiritual principles; it's about understanding and applying spiritual principles in the transformation of one's own nature, in service to the creation of a more peaceful, more beautiful world.

Spiritual development is an ongoing process and does not happen overnight. Be patient with yourself and take your time, but don't allow yourself to get lazy or justify lingering with dysfunctional behaviors. This does nothing but harm and hinder your process. Think about simple ways you can begin. When you'd like to make a change in your life, you have to make it as easy as possible at the beginning, almost like applying training wheels when learning to ride a bike. Before long, you'll be able to take off the training wheels and increase the difficulty and commitment.

A LIFESTYLE OF SETTING YOURSELF UP FOR SUCCESS

▶ Make every effort to live an orderly, comfortable, responsible life to provide your brain with rewards and reinforcement of healthy behaviors.

▶ Engage the body every single day through exercise, yoga, dancing, resistance training, or stretching.

▶ Learn different meditation techniques and practice them regularly. Introduce meditative consciousness throughout your day, infusing everyday actions like driving, eating, walking, and working with mindfulness. Bring it to social circumstances as well.

▶ Practice anticipatory self-care; don't wait until you're sick to take good care of yourself. Try not to let yourself get too tired, too hungry, or too lazy.

▶ Avoid drugs, alcohol, or other strong substances that can provide an unhealthy reward.

▶ Maintain healthy relationships with others that include reasonable boundaries and honest communication.

BREAKING THE CHAIN

In the Eastern traditions, it is said there are thousands of physical senses, but six major ones. The first five are the conventional senses of sight, touch, hearing, taste, and sound. The sixth sense? No, it's not intuition, telepathic abilities, or seeing the future. The sixth sense is thought. This is a very helpful perspective because we tend to give our thoughts extraordinary power—we typically believe what our thoughts tell us. However, when we look at our thoughts as sensory input—no different from the other five senses—we begin to re-contextualize our thinking mind altogether.

Our senses provide us with important data about the present moment. Imagine you're sitting on your couch reading a book and you begin to smell something burning. Because of your sense of smell, you are able to intervene. You put down the book, walk to the kitchen, and realize you forgot to set a timer for the cookies in the oven, which are now beginning to burn. In this scenario, there's not much to do with a dozen burnt cookies, but the situation could easily be more serious. The earlier you become aware of something harmful, the sooner you can intervene.

Now, look at your thoughts. As you begin to develop a more consistent meditation practice and a habit of observing your thoughts, you will find you become more sensitive to the subtleties in your thought life and able to intervene when unhelpful or dysfunctional thoughts first make themselves known.

To experience genuine self-transformation and truly move forward along the path of spiritual development, we must break the chain of command in our unwanted habits. This is done by interrupting the habit process through self-awareness. A daily practice of meditation will provide you with the self-awareness necessary to begin to catch your unhealthy thoughts and become more aware of your triggers earlier on, before they begin to activate the desires that lead to your negative responses and unwanted behaviors.

You and you alone can make these decisions for yourself, but in all of the great spiritual traditions, it is said that each and every one of us has access to and a relationship with one form or another of spirit guides. In Buddhism, we listen to our Buddha Nature. In Christianity, we are blessed by the comfort and guidance of the Holy Spirit. In the Indigenous traditions, the Great Spirit is available to support and lead us. In psychology, we speak of one's conscience. In the 12-step programs, a higher power is described who lives in us, but is not of us, who can do for us what we cannot do for ourselves. Whatever way you like to look at it, we have the opportunity to access spiritual guidance from within our hearts and minds that can help us invoke the supernatural power required to make the toughest decisions and overcome our greatest challenges.

In this chapter's exercise, we will attempt to engage the brain's plasticity, tune in to our higher wisdom, and overcome unwanted behaviors.

ENGAGING THE BRAIN'S PLASTICITY

The key to rewiring the brain is accessing neural plasticity. Neural plasticity is a natural quality of the brain, but to be applied, it must be engaged. Learning a new skill, instrument, or language is one of the best ways to engage the plasticity of the brain. Other ways to activate the brain's plasticity include getting to know a new environment, reading a challenging book, or working through puzzles. This makes it easier to establish new habits and adapt to new ideas and information.

INVOKING BREAKTHROUGH

The following exercise is designed to help you experience a sense of liberation from samsara, breaking the chains that keep you in unwanted cycles, and to reconnect you with your higher nature as a guide and source of power. You will plant seeds in your heart and mind that will help prepare you for transformation and success.

TIME 30 TO 60 MINUTES

WHAT YOU'LL NEED

- ▶ Journal and a pen
- ▶ Quiet, comfortable place with basic privacy
- ▶ Timer

OPTIONAL

You may choose to begin this practice with a prayer to invite the Holy Spirit or your spirit guides to support you in the noble cause of overcoming your lower nature. You may also choose to light white candles, wear white, play music, burn incense, or use essential oils to add a ceremonial quality to this exercise.

GET STARTED

1. Choose one particular unwanted behavior pattern you are prepared to let go of and overcome.

2. Get into a comfortable position you can maintain for the duration of the exercise.

3. Set a timer for 5 to 10 minutes, close your eyes, and begin by practicing a 20-second breath meditation using the instructions below. This will help slow the mind, bring you more deeply into the present moment, and relax your body so you can become more receptive to the next steps.

   ➤ Inhale for a count of five.

   ➤ Hold your breath for a count of five.

   ➤ Exhale for a count of five.

   ➤ Hold for a count of five.

4. Once your timer sounds, continue meditating without counting the breath. Every exhale should send a wave of relaxation through every part of your body, taking you into a deeper sense of relaxed stillness.

5. Once you have gotten into a relaxed meditative state, take a moment to communicate directly to your mind and body. Imagine you are speaking to every single atom of every cell in every part of your body and that in stillness, they can hear you clearly. Send love and gratitude. Feel free to use your words to communicate with your body and invite its support and partnership as you overcome your unwanted behaviors, or use these words as a guide:

   Thank you for everything. I love and accept you uncon-ditionally. I need your help now. Please let go entirely of the unwanted behavior of _____.

   ➤

Please eliminate the dysfunctional thoughts that support this behavior. Replace them with healthy thoughts. Please eliminate desires that support this behavior. Replace them with healthy desires. Together we can do this. Thank you.

6. Visualize every particle of your being agreeing to cooperate with you on the task to overcome this unwanted behavior.

7. Now, continue to meditate.

   ► For the duration of this meditation, silently repeat the mantra *imperium*, which means "power" or "authority." As you repeat it, visualize yourself making new decisions and taking new actions to replace the old unwanted behavior.

   ► Observe any thoughts or images that come to mind, breathing in and out, allowing the body to remain relaxed.

8. When you are ready to transition to the next phase, stand up and stretch your body in any way that feels comfortable for you. While you stretch, repeat the affirmation, "Breakthrough is coming." Say it as loud as you'd like, getting your whole nervous system involved. Feel it in your body and don't hold back.

WRAP UP

In your journal, describe the exercise, the different elements you added, time of day you practiced, and anything you felt throughout the process. Take your time writing about the new habits and behaviors you'll be engaging in that will replace your old, unwanted behavior, as if you are writing a "new story."

GO DEEPER

Incorporate these tools on a daily, consistent basis. The amount of time you spend in meditation is not in itself the important part; it is the quality and dedication to the practice that matters. Remember, we are working to perform a literal biological rewiring of the brain.

When you find yourself triggered in daily life:

- ➤ Practice the 20-second breath to help recalibrate your mind and body and give you more willpower to exercise self-control.
- ➤ Meditate using the mantra *imperium* to help you re-establish a sense of self-control.
- ➤ Take the affirmation "Breakthrough is coming" with you wherever you go—silently or quietly whispering it to yourself.

Move Through
Your Pain

WHEN WE HAVE A PHYSICAL wound, we must clean and disinfect it, apply the necessary ointments, and nurture it to allow the body's natural self-healing mechanism to kick in. The same is true about psychological wounds. To "disinfect" our psychological wounds is to make an effort to clear away any judgmental narratives that may be born from it, like, "Bad things always happen to me," or, "I'll never be good enough." Once "disinfected," we then have to nurture our wounds in just the right way. It can often be very healing to process your experiences with a loving friend. More often than not, we just need to have our pain witnessed. Then, the heart's natural self-healing mechanism will kick in.

When we facilitate the conditions for healing, the body knows what to do. Once we've taken care of a flesh wound, the most important thing to do is leave it alone, covered up and safe, to give the body a chance to heal; if you keep touching and prodding it, you increase the chances of infection. With emotional or psychological pain, dwelling on it or repeating it over and over can also prevent us from healing and keep our growth stagnant. We must do for the psyche and the heart what we do for the body—facilitate the conditions for healing and let time do what only time can do.

Dwelling on pain isn't the only way we keep it from healing. You might also keep a psychological wound open by focusing on mistakes from your past or pain you've caused others. But you don't need forgiveness from those you've hurt in order to grow. From a metaphysical perspective, once atonement has been activated, you can begin to move forward. The same goes for others. We can't wait for an apology from someone else before we allow ourselves to begin to heal. Healing is our job. Witness your pain yourself. Feel it. Experience it. Be fearless. Be brave. Be over it.

This doesn't invalidate your pain. Your pain is absolutely valid. We all go through hard, challenging, dark times in our lives, and without them, we would not be pushed to greater depths and higher heights. Some of the most extraordinary figures throughout history were once abused, tormented, and weakened by pain.

But a miracle happened within them, in their willingness to see beyond the pain, to see through the darkness to the light on the other side. No matter who caused your pain or where you learned your dysfunctional behavior, it's now yours to deal with.

Everyone Hurts

Society often provides dysfunctional messaging around emotional pain and processing. Reality TV, for example, isn't exactly known for showcasing healthy, functional adults who display mature emotional behavioral processing. But pain is a natural part of life.

In the Buddhist tradition, we learn that *dukka* is inherent to life experience. Dukka, for centuries, was translated as "suffering," though newer translations now refer to it as "frustration" or "resistance." Suffering, frustration, resistance, and challenges are part of life. We all have hurt we must move through. But know that pain is not without value. Through the metaphysical principle of contrast, we learn that without darkness, we would not appreciate light. Without sadness, we would not understand happiness. Without pain, we couldn't appreciate things such as joy, pleasure, contentment, and peace.

However, just because pain is normal does not mean it has to run your life. Normalizing suffering and recognizing it as a necessary part of the journey can help take away its power. It isn't that we want to minimize our pain; rather, we want to recognize that there will be a time when the pain is gone and you will be able to move on with your life.

In this chapter, you will learn to work through the pain, worry, hurt, and shame that might be standing between you and true fulfillment, genuine connection, and purpose. You will learn how to reconnect with your body and zoom out to find the larger lessons in your experiences.

PSYCHIC DIET

Just as your physical diet affects your body's ability to stave off infection, your psychic diet affects your heart's ability to heal. From a metaphysical and neuroscientific perspective, all our sensory input is digested by the mind—everything you watch, listen to, taste, touch, or smell enters into the unconscious, with microdata informing subtle ideas about you and the world in which you live.

Just as we must become aware of every word we speak and every thought we think, we must also become aware of our "psychic diet"—that is, everything we take in. Use mindfulness to tune in to your intuition and identify healthy content for your psyche to take in. Eliminate any music, TV, or social media personalities who bring immaturity, violence, hypersexuality, or other forms of dysfunction into your mind.

Ask yourself:

What do I watch, listen to, read, and otherwise expose myself to?

What messages am I unconsciously taking in?

What ways could this affect my mind, heart, and body?

ACKNOWLEDGE YOUR EMOTIONS

To truly move through pain, you must acknowledge the emotions associated with it. There is a pervasive notion in our culture that there is something wrong with expressing what we feel. Because of this idea, we often try to suppress uncomfortable or inconvenient emotions. Although it is sometimes valuable to find the right time or place to release and express your emotions or to analyze which emotions are immature or based on false pretenses, it is also crucial to recognize that the way you feel is valid and based on your current stage of consciousness. There is always a reason for what you feel. Allowing yourself to acknowledge what you feel is how you can find that reason.

This doesn't mean, though, that every time you have an emotional outburst it is right or warranted. But when it comes to the inner work, recognize that the pain came from somewhere. When we begin to look at our emotional experiences as chemical reactions or automatic unfoldings, we can disengage from emotional shame and examine their sources more effectively. Negative self-evaluation results in shame. Objective, mindful self-observation opens up the possibility of releasing unpleasant and negative emotions, allowing us to move forward.

Establishing a more enlightened relationship with our emotions means accepting ourselves as human. Don't compare your emotional process to another person's emotional process. Though all the same species, that doesn't mean we do things the same way. Through mindfulness, we can begin to identify changes in the body, shifts in the frequency or type of thoughts passing through our minds. Through that awareness, we can begin to self-regulate.

Reflect on the inner dialogue around your emotional process. Use the following questions as journal prompts to support and deepen your self-honesty:

- In what ways might you be isolating yourself emotionally?

- In what ways might you be withholding the expression of deeper feelings?

- In what ways might you be negatively self-evaluating or self-shaming?

- In what ways might you be justifying unnecessary or dysfunctional emotions?

- In what ways might you be willing to approach things differently?

RECONNECT TO YOUR BODY

Memories live in the body, through muscle memory and cellular memory. During negative or traumatic experiences, the body reacts, recoils, or resists, typically with a combination of muscle tension and hormone release. These reactions, though perfectly natural and normal, can cause a residual "whiplash" effect that remains in the body long after the negative experience has ended. Integrating these memories, clearing through their residue, and healing are all part of the higher nature's work in taming and overriding the lower nature.

These residual effects are sometimes called energy blocks. In Eastern medicine, we find many different approaches to removing energy blocks. This is based on the premise that the body's natural life force energy (chi, prana, reiki) flows intelligently to where it is needed most. In acupuncture, very small needles are placed into the skin at certain points, called meridians, to facilitate energy flow. These meridians are rivers of energy that can be blocked by physical injury, trauma, shame, and dietary deficiency.

Consider the ways in which trauma, drama, and shame live in your body. Are there parts of your body you are ashamed of or embarrassed by? To begin to tap into this, practice a body scan meditation. Lie flat on your back, get quiet, and allow the body to find stillness. Guide your attention to each part of your body, one body part at a time. Nonjudgmentally observe any physical sensations or thoughts that may arise. Notice especially the connection between any thoughts, memories, or images that arise simultaneously in concert with physical sensations. You don't need to analyze or "fix" anything; you just need to observe. Observing, or "bringing light," begins the natural process of healing.

Although this kind of body scan and open awareness practice can sometimes be uncomfortable, it can also be very relaxing and is a critical step toward accepting your body and feeling free from shame.

Yoga is the practice of calling the mind and body into deeper connection with one another. It also opens up energetic blockages by bringing together strength and flexibility throughout the body's muscles, tendons, and tissues, as well as detoxifying the organs. There are lots of different yoga practices, but any kind of physical activity that activates the mind-body connection will aid your higher nature in having more control over the body's functioning.

SEATED TORSO CIRCLES

This exercise is a simple way to stretch the spine and move energy throughout the body.

1. Sit cross-legged on the floor.

2. Rest your hands on or near your knees.

3. Rotate your torso a few times, circling your spine in a cone shape with the base of your spine as the apex of the cone. Lean your upper body down to the left, forward over your lap, up to the right, slightly backward, and then back to the left, continuing like so.

4. After a few minutes of rotating your torso to the left, begin to rotate in the other direction, to the right.

5. Practice slow, mindful movements, continuing to breathe deeply in and out for a few minutes. Observe the sensations in your body. You may also choose to close your eyes.

WORK THROUGH TRAUMA AND SHAME

Trauma is defined as any negative experience that brings the body and mind into a state of survival mode. Life-or-death situations (or circumstances that weren't actually life or death, but felt incredibly scary to you) are classified as traumatic. Experiences that have a negative emotion attached to them can sometimes be very dramatic and cause emotional pain, but are not technically considered traumatic.

Trauma, and the shame often associated with it, can be incredibly uncomfortable to talk about or even acknowledge. But if trauma remains unseen and unexplored, it continues to affect us and hold us back unconsciously. As we begin to explore our trauma and shame skillfully and with compassion, we can find relief in the simple fact we're no longer hiding from ourselves. Be courageous in the exploration of whatever trauma and shame you may be holding on to.

Psychologists say trauma affects the psyche in very sensitive ways, leading to possible personality disorders, abuse of self or others, addiction, and other negative responses. If you have a serious dramatic or traumatic experience you are processing, it's that much more important to be as gentle as possible with yourself and seek the support of a professional or specialist to work through it.

Transcend Emotional Pain

A friend and mentor was teaching me about wealth, money, building a business, and developing a career. We had a great brotherly bond and enjoyed one another's company. He seemed to have it all—a passport full of stamps, a supermodel wife, a beautiful mansion, a collection of very impressive cars . . . and he always seemed to be growing and changing. I loved to hear of all his adventures and receive his great advice.

One day, while he was in the midst of a challenging season, I received a call from his ex-wife, informing me he died by suicide. I had never seen his depression or sadness; he had never shown me that side of his life. I was stunned, devastated, and heartbroken. Everything changed for me in that moment. Not only did I commit to deepening my relationships with others so I might be a more present help in times of need, but I also took a deeper look at my own emotional pain.

Everyone has emotional pain—from the bravest, strongest, happiest person you know to the most sarcastic, harsh, superficial person you know. That means you do, too. But that doesn't mean you are broken, helpless, or lost. It just means you're human. What matters is what we do with what's been given to us.

Regardless of what you have done or what has happened to you in the past, there is nothing wrong with you. Look at the universe as a place of cause and effect. You, as a part of the universe, have a complex psyche co-created through the experiences you've had. The metaphysical principle of *karma* means that anything that exists is the result of causal factors. In a way, karma lets you off the hook for what you've done in the past and where you are today—as long as you're willing to interrupt the cycle and move on.

You now have the opportunity—and responsibility—to make a new choice and to do things differently. There are negative and positive beliefs we can unconsciously hold about emotional pain, and it is important to address our fears and anxieties to begin to move beyond them. Transcendence is about rising above your circumstances and beginning to see yourself, your emotions, and your life as part of a larger cosmic web. Allow yourself to expand, grow, and see things from a bigger perspective. Allow thoughts and questions about eternity to open your mind in meditation. Let go of the need to fully understand, explain, or control anything.

CONSCIOUS PLAYLIST

Your music choices are a part of your psychic diet that you should be especially aware of. The music we listen to can greatly affect our moods, in both conscious and unconscious ways. Create a playlist that supports feelings of enthusiasm, health, and optimism. Avoid anything that comes off as abrasive, harsh, despairing, violent, or crude. Keep your "psychic diet" in mind and select songs with uplifting lyrics, healing tones, and comfortable melodies.

LOOK FOR THE LESSON

As we continue on the path of personal spiritual development, we must always come back to the attitude of the positive onlooker. Even in the midst of challenging, uncomfortable, or painful experiences, there is something to be learned and gained. Train your mind to think this way by developing a habit of asking yourself, "What did I learn from that?" and "What can I learn from this?"

In more extreme circumstances, it can feel almost impossible to find a lesson. But those are the situations with the rawest power in them, and raw power can be directed and programmed with intention. In Indigenous cultures, someone who survives being struck by lightning is considered to have received a major dose of divine medicine intended to provide great healing and deep wisdom. Look at the drama and trauma that affects your life and open your mind to the possibility that the intensity of those challenges can be experienced as medicine from the universe.

Pain, though sometimes just awful and uncomfortable, can be an extraordinary gift of learning. There is strength in being vulnerable and power in being honest with ourselves. Resisting what we feel increases our suffering, whereas welcoming it is the path to inner peace.

Practice an act of conscious evolution by shifting your attention away from your pain, away from your thoughts, away from your goals and to-do list, and experience what it's like to *just be*. This allows your unconscious mind to experience the reality of the safety and peace available in the present moment, giving it space and time to shift and move things beneath the surface, softening pain and trauma into peace and stability.

In this exercise, you will acknowledge the reality of how you feel, while simultaneously tuning in to the great, miraculous cure for everything: faith. Faith will transform our fear into acceptance and hope and will open our hearts and minds to greater possibilities.

INVINCIBLE FAITH

TIME 30 TO 60 MINUTES

WHAT YOU'LL NEED

- ► Journal and pen
- ► Comfortable, private place to sit
- ► Timer

OPTIONAL

Explore spiritual music, cleaning and organizing your space before practicing the exercise, taking a shower, wearing something comfortable but spiritually significant, lighting candles, or burning incense and using essential oils. You may also choose to say a prayer as you begin to deepen your connection to your higher nature and set the intention for your practice.

GET STARTED

1. This Body Activation exercise will open the energy flow through the body's energetic meridians.

   - ► While seated, begin massaging each finger of both hands.

   - ► Open and close the fists, circle the wrists, and stretch the fingers.

   - ► Massage the muscles in your forearms, upper arms, and shoulders.

   - ► Roll your neck and shoulders in both directions a few times.

- ➤ Twist your spine by turning the body from the waist up to the left three to five times, then to the right three to five times.

- ➤ Extend your legs in front of you, massaging your thighs, your calves, and your feet.

- ➤ Rotate your ankles a few times in both directions, stretching your feet and toes.

2. Practice three Yogic Forward Folds to support energetic flow. If this is not possible, simply lean forward and backward to warm up the spine.

- ➤ Stand upright and extend your arms out straight to the left and right.

- ➤ Take a deep breath in and out. On your exhale, swan dive down into your first Forward Fold.

- ➤ Allow your hands to touch the floor, your ankles, your shins, or your knees, whatever is possible for your level of flexibility.

- ➤ Take a few deep breaths in and out in the fold before gradually beginning to roll back up, one vertebra at a time. Allow your back, shoulders, neck, and head to be the last things to come up out of the fold.

- ➤ Practice two more Forward Folds with exactly the same mindfulness and deep breaths.

➤

3. Finally, while seated, get still and practice meditation for 5 to 20 minutes. As you meditate, allow your inhales to stretch the lungs in all directions and your exhales to bring a wave of relaxation through every part of your body, calming the lower nature and relaxing your physical self.

   Silently repeat the mantra *omne remedium*, which means "the cure for everything" or "complete remedy." With every inhale, silently repeat the first part of the mantra, and with every exhale, silently repeat the second part of the mantra. Practice faith while visualizing the body, heart, mind, and spirit receiving the precise cure necessary.

4. When you've finished meditating, place your hands over your heart, take a deep breath in, and say, "Thank you, thank you, thank you . . . " as many times as you can with your exhale. Repeat this three times or more.

5. Begin to bring movement back into the body, standing up and stretching in any way that feels comfortable for you.

WRAP UP

Journal the images that came to mind, any spiritual guidance or intuitive impressions you may have received during the exercise, and any actions you feel inspired to take.

GO DEEPER

Introduce a daily practice of physical activity. It can be as simple as the Body Activation and Forward Folds, or you may choose to add additional Yogic postures or exercises such as push-ups, walking, or dancing. Remember, trying something new engages the brain's plasticity, making it more efficient at establishing new habits and patterns.

The Path to Positivity

GROWING UP, I HAD FAMILY dinners with my parents and four brothers. Every night, no one could have one bite of food until one of us had offered a blessing over that food. As soon as the prayer was over, we'd dig in, and at some point during just about every single meal of my childhood, my dad would say, "Is this living or what?!" In this and in other subtle ways, my dad displayed positive psychology, the principle of gratitude, and a recognition of what makes life worth living: the little things. You have to appreciate the good when you've got it.

Progressing forward on the journey of personal spiritual development is not always easy. We often find ourselves challenged by old beliefs, habitual thinking patterns, and the lifestyle we've grown comfortable with and accustomed to. One of the mental faculties that can best help us navigate these challenges is a positive mental attitude.

In addition to a new attitude, you will also need a realistic understanding of the values you currently live by and the likelihood that they are in stark contrast to the values you hold to be true in your heart. You'll need to look at your approach to self-care and infuse your new consciousness into your existing routine. Self-care is more than just anticipating your physical needs; it also involves keeping yourself in an emotionally balanced state through healthy boundaries, clear communication, and more.

In chapter 1, we discussed cultivating the attitude of the positive onlooker. Now, we deepen our understanding of what that means. We will also learn how to use gratitude and the Law of Attraction and Repulsion in our spiritual journey. The principles you learn in this chapter will help you live a more fulfilling, happier life, even in the face of uncertainty and discomfort.

A Brand-New Attitude

"You know, Ben, you're actually very gifted." I turned and looked at my mom, curious about what she had to say. "You've got a gift for calling out exactly what someone is insecure about and making a big deal about exactly what's not perfect in a situation. Ben, you've got a bad attitude!" It was true. As a teen, I, Ben Decker, had a bad attitude. I'd like to think my negative attitude didn't characterize my entire personality at the time, but I know it was there.

We all have a friend with a bad attitude. Whenever they're around, they seem to have a knack for finding fault with any person, place, or situation. Maybe, like me, you have some experience being that person.

On that long-ago day, it was what my mother said next that would echo in my mind forever: "You could learn to use your powers for good." And I did. I had to invoke the forces of reinvention and create a completely new version of myself to overcome my negative attitude and learn how to use my powers for good.

Positivity is not about being in easy, fun, or desirable circumstances. It's about inner resilience and adaptability. A child screams and cries to get the environment to change to suit them, whereas a psychologically healthy adult will adapt to navigate changes in their environment. Optimism comes from a deep sense that everything works out.

Cultivating a positive mental attitude doesn't happen overnight. It's more than putting on a fake smile to get through a frustrating or difficult situation. It's a reorientation of one's entire worldview. An attitude comes from within and radiates out, which means any adjustments to it must be deep, consistent, and authentic.

Making the conscious decision to walk along the spiritual path requires intentionally practicing mental flexibility: an active approach of thinking more deeply about things, while simultaneously allowing genuine optimism to inform all decisions.

The practice of a positive mental attitude can feel, quite literally, unnatural at first. There are legitimate challenges—physiological, circumstantial, emotional, and spiritual—we face as we establish our positive mental attitude. Fears and insecurities, memories of past problems, and images and ideas we've unconsciously absorbed through media and relationships can flood our mind and make it seem impossible to see things differently, positively. You do not have to believe these automatic thoughts. Your past is not a prophecy of your future. You have the power to create a new thought. You can disrupt the habitual patterns you have demonstrated and create a new foundational consciousness.

Keep in mind that the more you exercise your ability to see things differently, the more your body and brain will become conditioned to do so. As we learned in chapter 2, this will gradually and naturally reinforce the habit.

Take a moment to reflect on your attitude. When someone asks you about your day, do you find yourself complaining or expressing gratitude and enthusiasm? In group discussions, do you find yourself being agreeable or disagreeable? These are attitudinal considerations. Difficult circumstances can present themselves to you throughout your day, but you do not have to complain about them. You can disagree without being disagreeable.

As you reflect on the general state of your attitude, bring your awareness to your breath. You may notice that you naturally tend to hold your breath. This is a normal automatic response to thinking about something uncomfortable, as tension in the body is a normal reaction to discomfort. Allow your body to relax. Let go of any self-judgment or self-criticism. This is an assessment of your current attitudinal state so you can have a realistic idea of the next right steps to take. No matter the experiences that have contributed to your current attitudinal state, there are many things you can do to overcome the brain's biases and sustain positive change.

PRONOIA

Paranoia is the extreme expression of the mind's negativity bias and a feeling that the universe is conspiring against us and trying to cause us harm. "Pronoia" is the opposite, the expression of the mind's positivity bias, a belief that the universe around us is conspiring to help us in every way possible. Meditate on the idea that everything is happening for you. Practice pronoia as you cultivate the attitude of the positive onlooker.

BE A MAGNET FOR GOOD

The Eastern concept of *karma* is the universal metaphysical law of cause and effect as applied to our personal lives. Typically, we move about the world with a general sense that everything is separate, that if we "don't get caught" doing a specific thing, then we are off the hook. From a metaphysical perspective, everything is interconnected and no action, word, or thought is without its matching effect. What we generate comes back to us.

At its deepest level, the law of karma calls us to the reflection of who we are. We don't attract or create what we "try" to attract or create. We get what we give. We see what we are. This goes back to the understanding of our fundamental nature as eternal spiritual beings having a temporary human experience.

My grandmother—who actually named my mom Karma—taught me about the principle of karma when I was just a child. Grandma loved to garden with us. She especially loved planting bulbs because they grew back every season. Planting tulip and daffodil bulbs in fertile soil is like offering gifts of loving-kindness to others. When we are loving and generous with others, we experience the spirit of love and generosity coming back to us through the cycle of samsara, as referred to in chapter 2.

Grandma also taught us that when we see weeds in the garden, we must pull them up from the root, rather than just cutting off that which can be seen above the surface. Doing the extra work to pull the weed up may take more time and energy now, but it ultimately saves energy and generates good karma because that weed will not grow back. However, taking the easy way out by simply cutting off the visible portion of the weed will generate negative karma—with its roots still in the ground, that weed will easily grow back as a reminder of what has not been taken care of.

The cultivation of patience is crucial. We must know that a perfectly tended garden is not an immediate manifestation, but something carefully cultivated and consistently maintained. The same is true about the quality of our spirits. Human life is a spiritual initiation wherein we learn, expand, and grow into more evolved versions of ourselves. The universe loves progression, evolution, and expansion, and it rewards these things.

Open your mind to seeing things differently. Consider that you are not the victim or the innocent bystander of the experiences in your life, but instead that you are co-creator of your experiences. Look around you. Notice where you are, what surrounds you, and what is happening. From a metaphysical perspective, all these things radiate from deep within you, outward in all directions. What do you project into the world? What do your relationships, circumstances, and surroundings reflect back to you? Journal about this and be honest with yourself— but don't be hard on yourself.

THE LAW OF ATTRACTION AND REPULSION

The Law of Attraction and Repulsion shows us that when we want something, the work is to become the right magnetic pairing for it. When we want to have or experience something, we often act out of desperation, which is a vibrational emphasis on our *difference* from the thing we want. This repels it.

Meditate on the energetic and vibrational essence of the goodness, wholeness, and purity you want to experience. Allow yourself to *become it*. This is what will manifest the abundance, joy, and love you seek.

DEFINE YOUR "WHAT" AND YOUR "WHY"

Defining your "what" means powerfully articulating your intention. An "intention" is an "invocation of a tendency." Tendencies are the general direction we push the skills we develop. In life, it is rarely about one skill but, rather, a lifestyle of skills that gets us where we want to go. A successful painter isn't skilled only in the stroke of the brush, but in the mixing of color, in visualizing something new, and in the follow-through. An artist has a tendency toward beauty–the beauty of each stroke, the beauty of perfectly mixed color, the beauty of something new, and the beauty of a finished project.

Defining your "why" is about identifying the source of the deeper passion beneath your "what."

This isn't about pretending to be something you are not; it's about recognizing the reality of your current state of consciousness so you can effectively work to learn and grow from that place to the next, higher phase in your evolutionary journey. Reflect on the reality that has drawn you to the path of spiritual development. Take time to meditate on the below questions. Summarize your answers into strong, direct statements, like the examples following.

1. What skills do I seek to cultivate?

2. Why am I committed to this path?

Your answers might be something like, "I seek to heal, overcome, and evolve," or, "I am committed to my spiritual path because of my deep understanding and faith that this will bring fulfillment and joy."

Revisit your answers to these questions when your spiritual development work becomes challenging.

THE NEUROSCIENCE OF FAITH

Faith is a profound sense of openness and trust that unlocks the possibility of new neural pathways to open and be established. Prayer is the articulation that guides the direction of those new neural pathways. So, miracles are the result, or effect, of the two.

Being "open to receiving a miracle," is another way of saying, "I am open to a completely new mapping of neural pathways that can reorient my perspective in this situation, to see it and relate to it completely differently."

Live Your Values

Although happiness is important, it isn't required to adopt a more positive mindset. Inner harmony is the key to releasing inner conflict and opening the possibility for positivity. This is achieved in moments when our values, our feelings, and our behaviors are in tune.

To live in integrity with ourselves, we must identify those values that are most important to us. There are two steps to doing this. First, recognize that the default values our behaviors actually reveal are important to us. In this first step, we must look at what motivates us in our relationships, our work, and our decision-making. This is usually highly influenced by the consciousness of the world around us, so it is sometimes not pretty. Be fearless as you examine that which has shaped your motivation.

Second, identify that which we value in a deeper, truer sense. What are the values and qualities that motivate and inspire you in a deeper sense? What are the things your heart desires for others? For the world?

Everything is connected. From a karmic perspective, realize that the decisions you make and the actions you take from the default value system generate negative karma. When we live with a mental attitude focused only on personal gain, we generate negative karma. When we allow our ego to make moves for us, we generate negative karma.

Our value system must be based on the universal principle of unity and interconnectedness. The aphorism, "If it's happening anywhere, it's happening to me," rings true metaphysically and provides a clue to higher values. It means both your pain and someone else's pain are important. Discomfort with this process is normal, as the thinking of our higher nature is exactly opposite from the thinking of our lower nature. The lower nature wants to hoard and withdraw, whereas the higher nature wants to share and embrace.

Consider your values when it's time to make a difficult decision. Consider your values when you find yourself impatient, angry, frustrated, jealous, or bitter. What are some ways you can demonstrate your values in real-life circumstances? Create reminders for yourself about your values. Find songs, programs, books, support groups, activities, and social media accounts that support your core values. The Psychic Diet (see page 36) and Conscious Playlist (see page 42) will help you plant the seeds of your core values into your subconscious, giving them a chance to gradually break through the rigidity of your default value system, creating a new mind and a new life altogether.

LIVE MY VALUES

In your journal, create two columns. On the left write "Default," and on the right, write "Conscious." In the left column, list the fears, worries, insecurities, and anxieties that motivate your actions. In the right column, write the positive values you believe in your heart that you would like to integrate more deeply as you raise your consciousness.

Nurture Your Inner Self

A key part of this journey is cultivating actionable skills to help you persevere on the path to positivity. Examine your lifestyle and be open to changing any aspect of it. If you are serious about putting your life in the hands of your higher self, you need to practice total surrender and trust the guidance of your higher self, even when your lower nature or ego wants to keep you stagnant. Your ego will not like it, but your higher self will lead you to new places and faces that will give you experiences you'd never know without that risk of surrender. Stay vigilant. Stay dedicated. Study yourself and determine what it means for you to increase your momentum and consistency.

Seek and find relationships that nurture the inner work you are doing. Surround yourself with honest people of integrity. Start by seeing the best in those around you now. Don't throw them away hoping to find new friends. Begin by loving those in your life today. Practice seeing every person you encounter through the eyes of your higher self, remembering the great principle of unity. Practice seeing divinity in others and you will begin to see divinity in yourself. As you begin to authentically increase your love and acceptance of those around you, you will find that some people may rotate out of your life for a time. That is okay. Remember, they are on their own journey and they are permitted, through divine birthright, to create their own destiny.

Develop techniques for self-care that are right for you. Sometimes, we let our personal care slide for so long that we lower our standards for how we show up for ourselves and others. Get real, get grounded, and get honest with yourself about what you need to do to feel your best and show up for the world as your best.

It is also common to have unconscious beliefs that tell us spending extra time getting ready is unnecessary or wasteful (and depending on what you're doing, it certainly can be). But done right, those extra few intentional moments can make all

the difference in your world. Remember, everything is connected. That means that, yes, taking good care of your body
and getting enough rest are part of a spiritual practice—but
please know it does not stop there.

Self-care isn't only about personal care routines. Healthy
boundaries in our relationships can help us avoid overcommit-
ting and underdelivering or allowing others to sap too much of
our resources. Conversely, nurturing your true self also involves
getting your hands dirty from time to time—getting involved,
participating in the community, and rising to the occasion when
society needs it. Notice areas in your life where you may have a
habit of dishonesty, laziness, or disorder. These are telltale signs
of weak boundaries. Begin by being honest with yourself and
others about how you feel. Do it with love. You'd be surprised
how easy it is to have your needs met when you communicate
clearly with love and integrity. You'd also be surprised at how
fulfilling it is to make a real difference in your community.

Finally, when things don't go your way, bounce back. Always
do your best, but when the outcome doesn't turn out as you
planned or how you'd like, don't wallow in it. Rise up. Be strong.
And, I don't mean to be insensitive, but get over it. Practice
tough love with yourself, if you need to. You are a powerful
creature with an extraordinary destiny, and resilience is a must.

Cultivate resilience through meditation. Meditation is not
about sitting down for a rote ritualistic practice; it's about working consciously with the brain, the nervous system, the body,
the emotions, and the spirit to create psychological resilience
and optimize the functioning of the body and mind. At its best,
meditation helps train us to become more conscious and more
receptive to the voice of our higher natures, while optimiz-
ing the body's ability to heal itself, thus becoming a greater
attractive force for positivity in our lives. We do this by infusing
meditative consciousness into other activities, like eating, drinking, and personal care.

METAPHYSICAL SELF-CARE

There are three primary components of metaphysical self-care: infusing normal personal care activities, like showers, with mindfulness, then applying symbolic psychological or spiritual meaning to the activity, and making sure to perform the activity consistently, in a way that integrates comfortably into daily living.

This exercise is designed to take you through an activity and help rewire your brain and nervous system. It will support your efforts to establish a positive mental attitude, attract more goodness into your life, and care more deeply for your inner self. We'll use a shower for this example, but feel free to substitute any other self-care activity.

TIME   30 TO 60 MINUTES

WHAT YOU'LL NEED

- ▶ Journal and pen
- ▶ Bathroom where you normally bathe or shower
- ▶ Your "what" and "why" from earlier in this chapter (see page 55)
- ▶ Timer

OPTIONAL

You may choose to create a sacred space to practice your exercise with prayer, candles, music, incense, etc. to help you. Give yourself extra time, if possible, and enjoy the process—it's about rewiring your brain through the deliberate creation of a meaningful experience.

1. Consider the various aspects of your morning shower routine and write them in your journal. Note the process of your shower, what products you use, and what it may symbolize for you. Emphasize purification, putting your best foot forward through thorough self-care, and attracting goodness into your life.

2. Revisit your "what" and "why." Write them in your journal.

3. Write these three mantras and their meanings:

   ➤ *Tempora nova*, which means "new era," "new season," or "new times"

   ➤ *Nova mentis*, which means "new mind"

   ➤ *Vita nova*, which means "new life"

4. Clean your bathroom, clear out any clutter, and make an effort to create a sense of organization, clarity, and even beauty in the space.

5. Notice anything that might have unhealthy imagery or negativity associated with it, such as a fashion magazine that makes you feel insecure. Get rid of it.

6. Take a moment to consider your "what" and "why," possibly saying them aloud a few times.

7. As you get ready to take a shower, repeat the mantra *tempora nova*—silently or aloud, whichever is comfortable for you—to help signify and communicate to your unconscious that something new is occurring.

➤

8. Begin your shower and allow the warm water to rinse every part of your body. Breathe deeply, relax, and practice mindfulness; notice the lighting, the temperature, the sensations, the smells.

9. Imagine any negativity, stress, anxiety, or character defects being washed away by the water. Continue to repeat the mantra *tempora nova*.

10. As you wash your hair, massage your scalp and repeat the mantra *nova mentis*, sending the message to your brain that you are open to a completely new way of seeing things.

11. As you dry off your body, repeat the mantra *vita nova*, visualizing how you'd like to feel, behave, and operate today. Imagine your "new life" with your positive mental attitude and living authentically from your higher values.

WRAP UP

In your journal, describe the exercise you did, the different elements you added, the time of day you practiced, and anything you felt throughout the process.

GO DEEPER

You just engaged in the first phase of metaphysical self-care, *induction*, which is about setting up the foundation for the future.

In the next phase, *maintenance*, you'll conduct this ritual daily, doing it more efficiently, simplifying it, and adapting it to fit your daily routine. The idea is to make metaphysical living as grounded and realistic as possible—not to make every shower an elaborate exercise, but to be *mindful*, *present*, and *intentional*—even in small, quick moments.

The third phase, *recalibration*, occurs when your routine begins to lag and you've let go of the visualizations or forgotten your "what" or your "why." Recalibrate by refilling your supplies and giving yourself a little extra time to complete the full exercise again, reminding yourself of the mantras, practicing the visualization, and being completely present with the experience.

Get to Know
Your Heart

ANCIENT EGYPTIANS TOLD THE STORY of Ma'at, the
archetypal representation of the universal forces of balance,
harmony, truth, and justice. She stands at the gates where humans
transition from life to death. Everyone who leaves the Earth plane
meets Ma'at in the underworld, where she weighs the purity of
your soul by placing your heart on one end of a balance scale and
a feather on the other. If your heart is pure, it will be as light as a
feather and you can then move on to a heavenly afterlife.

We can learn from the wisdom of this ancient tale and apply
it to our lives today. When ignored, normal life experiences like
guilt, grief, and pain become heavy. The heaviness of the heart
can weigh down our souls and keep us from moving through life
with joy. If our hearts are heavy with unprocessed, unreleased,
unintegrated challenging life experiences, our heart cannot do
what it is designed to do: provide us great wisdom and insight.

In this chapter, you will get closer to the core of who you
really are and learn to experience the wisdom of your heart. You

will tune in to the energetic cords tied to your heart and follow them where they lead to begin to understand your beliefs, strengths, shortcomings, and motivations. Positive psychology, as well as spirituality, are as concerned about repairing and healing from our shortcomings and trauma as they are about cultivating and developing our strengths, hopes, and dreams.

The spiritual journey requires deep personal purification, the forgiveness of our shortcomings, and renunciation of our character defects, as well as the integration of new ways of operating in the world. From a metaphysical perspective, faking it, performing, or pretending won't do. The change cannot happen on a behavioral level alone, though that is crucial. It must come from within.

THE CORE OF WHO YOU ARE

Whether you want to call it your spirit heart, higher nature, or essence, getting to know your inner self is critical to understanding your purpose, values, vision, goals, motivations, and beliefs. Even though it is often unconscious, the fundamental nature of your existence informs what you do and how you do it. That's why understanding it is incredibly important.

As I've mentioned, the core fundamental principle in this book is that you are a child of the universe. What does it mean to be the "child" of something? A bear cub, if it lives a healthy life safe from harm, grows into a full-grown adult bear. An acorn, given the right circumstances and conditions, gradually, naturally, eventually becomes a full-blown oak tree. As we grow, taking good care of ourselves, making wise decisions, listening to the still, small voice within, we, too, become more like that which birthed us into existence.

Your identity is not what others have told you, nor what you believe about yourself. There is an inherent reality that is universal, true, and unchangeable. To unlock the power that lies in our divine nature, we have to be truly open to a genuine experience with it. From a Buddhist perspective, humanity is a process through which spiritual evolution takes place. In some Buddhist schools of thought, it is believed that every individual ego literally incarnates and reincarnates into many different bodies over time to learn and process through increasingly complex life challenges. From a metaphysical perspective, we must remember the foundational principle of the unity of all things. That implies that the teachings of reincarnation can be considered a parabolic lesson in unity consciousness.

Spiritually speaking, there is one life and infinite points of view. This indicates that the doctrine of past lives can be integrated into our awareness through the understanding that life is genuinely never-ending. It can be interpreted as an implication that I am you in a future life, that you and I live parallel lives, that we are one underneath the temporary veil of the body. The teaching of reincarnation can help us reflect more deeply on what it must be like to be another person, to walk a lifetime in another's shoes in completely different circumstances.

We find a similar teaching in the Judeo-Christian-Islamic lineage that refers to all people as brothers and sisters, another indicator of unity. Of course, we are not literally brothers and sisters and perhaps our separate ego identities are not literally incarnated and reincarnated, but rather our ancient ancestors did their best to teach us compassion, love, and unity through these perspectives of personal identity.

BEHOLD YOUR BELIEFS

To follow up on the belief-centered work we did in chapter 1, revisit the state of your beliefs. Take some time to identify new and true beliefs that match up with your heart and your most authentic self. Write about these beliefs in your journal. Explore the ways in which these new beliefs compare to the beliefs you held previously about yourself.

Recognize Your Strengths

Now that you have gained more clarity on the core of who you are, think about your strengths. What are you good at? What skills or talents come naturally to you? Your natural strengths may not be things that intrigue or interest you. Although your strengths are only part of who you are, tapping into them can help you create a more well-rounded picture of yourself. In what areas of your life do your strengths demonstrate themselves? In what ways do you use or apply your strengths? Do others benefit from your strengths and gifts?

What do your strengths tell you about your nature? Meditate on these strengths. Remember and imagine the ways they play out in your life and how they affect the lives of others, keeping in mind the principle of unity consciousness. What ways can your gifts be applied to benefit others? Our strengths only represent a portion of our identity, but having an objective, healthy idea of our strengths establishes a grounded sense of confidence, which can increase our capacity for decision-making and overcoming shortcomings.

There are areas in our lives where we are capable and other areas where we are gifted. Take a moment to identify three qualities or strengths that may fall under these three categories:

1. **Capable:** This is an area in which you take care of things with a reasonable level of skill that many people can match.

2. **Skilled:** This describes a talent or skill you have refined and in which you have developed an above-average proficiency.

3. **Gifted:** This refers to the areas where you are naturally very strong and hardly have to try to be great. Everyone is gifted in one way or another.

GOOD/BAD VERSUS ORDERLY/DISORDERLY

Mindfulness practice helps us realize subtleties that go deeper than the notion that something is "good" or "bad." Practice nonjudgment, opening your mind to seeing things with a sense of curiosity and nuance, beyond judgmental analysis.

Instead of being "bad," something may be:

➤ Disorderly

➤ Ignorant

➤ Immature

➤ Underdeveloped

Instead of "good," something may be:

➤ Knowledgeable

➤ Mature

➤ Orderly

➤ Refined

What are some things you think of as "bad"? Could it be possible they are actually the result of immaturity, ignorance, or disorder? Journal about your reflections and any insights that arise.

Forgive Your Shortcomings

Another key part of accessing our core selves involves recognizing and forgiving our shortcomings with gentleness and nonjudgment. There is a tendency to operate on a polarized scale of self-assessment: being either too lenient with ourselves, allowing ourselves to get away with too much, or too hard on ourselves, never giving ourselves a chance to make a mistake. As they say in the Buddhist traditions, we need to find the "middle path," where we move through our self-talk with balance.

Think about your shortcomings, failures, or anything else that needs forgiveness. Are they mistakes you made out of anger, jealousy, or insecurity? Or are your shortcomings born of laziness, inexperience, or ignorance? Open your mind to seeing yourself as a living being, moving gradually though a great, elaborate process.

These shortcomings contribute to who you are. It is not perfection that makes us valuable, lovable, or worthy of joy. These shortcomings are likely to be balanced by the strengths we identified in the previous section. Consider yourself as a living being in a great process of physical, spiritual, and psychological evolution. Disengage from self-judgment and tune in to self-observation. Be inspired by those who are strong in areas where you are not, but do not be discouraged. Practice a sense of self-acceptance, with recognition that you are always changing, always transforming, with the power to adapt, heal, and grow.

Because we all have shortcomings and we all make mistakes, learning to laugh at your mistakes is important. The practice of not taking yourself too seriously will contribute to your ability to cultivate resilience. As Christ was known to have said more than once after performing a miracle, "You are forgiven, go and sin no more." That essentially means: *Hey, it's in the past. You're good now. It's all good. Don't do it again.* Softening our self-judgment can also help us soften our judgment and criticism of others. It is a quality of an immature mind to want to attack and break down someone else. A mature mind wants to inspire, uplift, and bless.

Negative self-talk seems to have an especially powerful tone and we often find ourselves believing what our negative bias has to say. We can observe harsh negative self-talk by practicing mindfulness-based meditation. Witness the different thoughts that arise in the mind and allow the body to relax. You will begin to notice that the nervous system has subtle responses as certain thoughts make themselves known.

When you make a mistake, don't avoid the negative feeling that surrounds it. Breathe into it. Let yourself experience those feelings of regret and disappointment. This is part of our psychological immune system purging us of that error, providing the psychological medicine we need. Breathe. Allow yourself to feel all of it. Honor the reality of how you feel. Then, let it go.

If you have those good friends who will side with you no matter how immature or ignorant your actions and perspective may be, take it up with your higher self, if possible, before bringing it to others. You will be able to see the situation in a way that people who want to protect you might struggle with.

METAPHYSICAL AMENDS

We practice transforming the way we see the world and we practice transforming the way we interact with the world. Part of that practice is recognizing the ways we may have harmed others and making efforts toward genuine amends. Even something small—a misunderstood statement or a careless act of dishonesty—can leave an energetic rift in our relationships.

▶ Meditate and be extra compassionate with yourself.

▶ Meditate on the personal characteristics that made it possible for harm to be done. Be willing to overcome them.

▶ Meditate on what it would mean to seek amends.

▶ Visualize amends being made and breathe through it until you feel peaceful.

You will find that something in the air will be altered, the relationship will begin to adjust, tides will begin to turn, and seasons will begin to change.

Honor Your Hopes and Dreams

What is it that gets you out of bed in the morning? What do you think about when you daydream? The answer to these questions may surprise you. Often, we have judgments against our goals—and those judgments are typically a combination of wise discernment and harsh criticism. Let go of the harsh criticism and tune in to the wise discernment. What is it about your dreams that really motivates you?

Many of us have dreams of increasing our wealth and resources. There tends to be, either, an overemphasis on wealth or an overemphasis on the internalized belief that wealth is inherently bad. Find the middle path. In its purest essence, wealth is some-thing that indicates a deeper desire for greater self-expression and fulfillment, which is not a bad thing at all. As you progress on the spiritual path, you will gradually and naturally release the more superficial layers of your hopes, dreams, and goals, but just as with our shortcomings, we must first observe them, breathe into them, and allow ourselves to honor their reality.

Yes, you will likely have a few hopes and dreams that are unhealthy, unspiritual, and unwise. That's okay. Don't suppress them. Breathe into them. Accept yourself as you are now, never forgetting that life's journey is about transformation. Your hopes and dreams are not stagnant; they evolve as your conscious-ness evolves.

You will also likely have hopes and dreams so simple they may surprise you. Look deep within and observe the thoughts and feelings that really feel good to you. Take note of the images or ideas that come to mind. You may have an image of a happy family around the dinner table or a longing for a partner who loves you just as you are. We all have thousands of hopes and dreams, and all of them should be observed and honored, but there are a few that come from a deeper place within our-selves that will survive the test of time.

Our hopes and dreams give our lives meaning and purpose. They connect us to a larger timeline and greater possibilities. They add nuances to your journey that no one else will ever understand, and it is designed that way. Allow yourself the time and space to sit with your feelings, to really observe your heart's desires. You may even choose to practice a meditation using the mantra, "What do I want?" Witness the automatic responses the mind provides without any criticism. Just observe. Allow your own higher self to sort through that which is good, healthy, and wise. Relax, allow, and observe. What comes up for you?

Now, take a moment to consider the future. Where do you see yourself in five years? Ten? Twenty? In what ways are you currently honoring and working to realize your hopes and dreams?

HOPES, DREAMS, AND CORE VALUES

The following exercise is designed to establish a deep sense of faithfulness in your own true core values, while bringing lightness into your heart.

TIME   30 TO 60 MINUTES

WHAT YOU'LL NEED

- ➤ Journal and a pen
- ➤ Comfortable place to sit where you won't be interrupted
- ➤ Timer

OPTIONAL

Feel free to add more meditation time, relaxing music, a shower or bath beforehand, and other symbolically significant elements to increase the meaning of the exercise for you.

GET STARTED

1. Take a comfortable seated position and place both hands over your heart. Visualize a spark of white light growing larger and larger from the deepest core of your being. Maintain this visualization for the duration of the meditation.

2. Every exhale will have two parts: sending a wave of relaxation through every part of your body, then silently repeating the mantra *semper fidelis,* which means "always faithful." Continue this practice for 5 to 20 minutes.

3. Set your timer again for 5 to 20 minutes, this time for writing. Write in your journal until your timer sounds, using the following questions as prompts:

   ▶ What hopes and dreams do I have that are faithful to my core values?

   ▶ What goals do I have that are in alignment with these hopes and dreams?

   ▶ What can I put into action today to take me closer to these goals?

4. Set your timer for 5 to 20 minutes more.

5. Meditate again with your hands over your heart, using the mantra *semper fidelis* and the visualization of white light radiating from the core of your being.

WRAP UP

Write about the exercise in your journal, the different elements you added, the time of day you practiced, and anything you felt throughout the process. Look at your journal notes as if you were a scientist performing an experiment. Keep the relevant information about the practice and experience for yourself so you can measure and track how you felt, what you intended, and what changed.

GO DEEPER

Revisit this practice when you need a reconnection to your heart or when you need to reinvigorate your enthusiasm around your hopes and dreams.

Tap into Your True Self

A CLIENT ONCE TOLD ME she was very unhappy with her husband. They had been married for several years and their connection had been fading for a while. He came home late from work one night and seemed on edge. There was no food in the house and he hadn't eaten all day. As she described the argument that came next, when he ranted about his bad day and how frustrating it was for him that there was nothing to eat, she said, "He really showed his true colors."

When someone does something unkind or harsh, we sometimes say they have "shown their true colors," implying all the love and kindness we have experienced from them in the past was just an act and who they really are was revealed in a moment of anger or frustration.

But you are not who you are when you are angry, upset, hungry, or tired. You are not who you are when you are depleted, stretched too thin, and overwhelmed. Those are the times when our lower nature, or ego, takes over and says and does things we often later regret. Your true nature, or "true colors," reveals itself when you are rested, patient, and connected to your higher self. There is certainly a difference between a rift and abuse, but in most cases, a rift is just a rift.

In this chapter, we will practice seeing things from a bigger perspective, understanding our needs, and developing a relationship with the two voices within: that of the ego and that of our higher selves.

CULTIVATE A BIRD'S-EYE VIEW

Context is everything. Zooming out and viewing our life from afar can help us understand our own dramas, stories, and circumstances with humility and softness. The skill of being able to see things from a bigger perspective allows us to take in the entirety of a situation. Imagine watching a TV show and only being able to see 10 minutes of the 33rd episode. You wouldn't understand the context, the scene, the characters, or their motivation. When we cultivate a bird's-eye view, we bring more truth into our awareness, reducing our ignorance, and providing more data from which to make decisions.

Developing a broader perspective can be challenging at times, especially when there is pain, discomfort, or disappointment involved. However, the feelings of pain, discomfort, and disappointment are the precise signals that indicate the need to step back and see the situation for what it really is. The ego likes to stay small, but the observer takes in the bigger picture with ease.

The greatest challenge that comes with cultivating a bird's-eye view in a difficult situation is not the discomfort of the actual moment itself, but having to face the possibility that we are wrong or that we didn't understand the situation completely. My friend often says, "The quickest way to win an argument is to admit you're wrong." This is good practice to put into place, but once we know we're wrong, it becomes very difficult to return to our old ways of being.

Imagine you're holding a fresh orange. Now, imagine taking a nice big bite of that juicy orange, sinking your teeth into it and letting the juices flood your mouth. You will notice that your mouth has begun to water, even though the orange is not real, it is only imagined.

Now, call to mind your most present challenge—use the first challenge, problem, or goal that comes to mind. See yourself in that situation and allow your awareness to expand. Imagine growing larger and larger, but your goal or problem or circumstance stays the same size. Continue to "look down" until your problem seems to get smaller and smaller as your vision takes in more and more context, until you can hardly see the problem at all. Come back to this practice when you feel overwhelmed. Just as your mouth watered at the thought of biting into a fresh orange, your body and mind will adapt to the message of you being much larger than the challenges you face.

ANTICIPATE YOUR EGO

Our lower nature has a voice associated with it. That voice goes by many names: ego, mind, lower mind, etc. It is the voice of separation and it represents disconnection from all things. The ego voice exists to protect us from harm and help us survive. However, it is heavily conditioned by past experiences, fears, and social expectations. Any thought that operates from the premise of disconnection from the surrounding world is born of the ego.

In some circumstances, the ego provides important survival responses to keep us on track. But the ego is also quick to judge and discriminate, and can sometimes be our worst enemy. Consistent self-care will help the ego stay satiated and relaxed so the voice of your higher self can be heard clearly.

By contrast, your higher nature, or your observer, will reflect on things with more nuance. Rather than acting discriminating and impetuous, the observer is discerning and thoughtful. The ego likes to react immediately, whereas the observer takes a moment to process and respond thoughtfully.

Sometimes, we can easily identify when the ego is taking over—like when we find ourselves enraged, jealous, or overly emotional. Other times, it's not so easy. Here are a few ways to identify the voice of the ego:

- ► The ego delivers rapid-fire thoughts and ideas, one after another. Do your thoughts quickly flood your mind?

- ► The ego is characterized by a premise of separation. Review the messages from your thoughts. Do they further separate you from others?

- ► The ego operates primarily from a place of fear, anger, bitterness, and insecurity. Does the voice you hear have any of these qualities in the undertone of its message to you?

When you find that your thoughts are ego-derived, take a few deep breaths. Allow your body to relax. This will calm your nervous system and send a message to the ego that you hear it and will consider its message. As the tension in your body settles, it will become easier for you to observe the experience in the present moment, helping you feel at ease and think more clearly.

MASLOW'S HIERARCHY OF NEEDS

Psychologist Abraham Maslow developed a theory about what drives humanity, referred to as Maslow's Hierarchy of Needs. He designed a pyramid-shaped diagram. The bottom of the pyramid represents the most basic needs of every living thing. As the pyramid progresses toward the top, the needs become more advanced and refined.

At the top of the pyramid, we find the capstone: transcendence. The seven layers below transcendence are self-actualization, aesthetic needs, cognitive needs, esteem needs, belonging and love needs, safety needs, and physiological needs. The bottom half of the diagram represents what are referred to as "deficiency needs"; the top half represents "growth needs." This means anything on the bottom half of the diagram is absolutely necessary for a normal, functioning human life; anything on the top half exists within a more aspirational, expansive context of personal expression and evolution.

Maslow's Hierarchy of Needs loosely parallels the chakra system. The chakras are wheels of energy associated with different sectors of the body and different experiences in life, based on the biological and glandular associations. For example, the second chakra, the sacral chakra, is associated with the sexual organs and, therefore, sexuality and creativity. The top chakra, the crown, is associated with transcendence and divine inspiration, just like the capstone on Maslow's Hierarchy of Needs. The base chakra, the root, is associated with needs related to basic survival, similar to the base of Maslow's pyramid. Those in between have a gradual quality of increasing that parallels Maslow's. Some even believe Maslow was inspired by the Yogic chakra system in his creation of the Hierarchy of Needs.

MASLOW'S PYRAMID AND THE SEVEN CHAKRAS

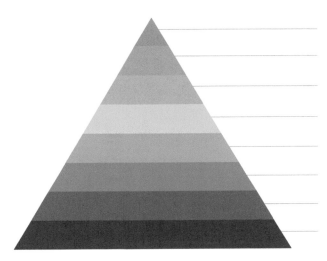

TRANSCENDENCE

SELF ACTUALIZATION

AESTHETIC NEEDS

COGNITIVE NEEDS

ESTEEM NEEDS

BELONGING AND LOVE NEEDS

SAFETY NEEDS

PHYSIOLOGICAL NEEDS

SAHASTRARA CHAKRA
CROWN CHAKRA

AJNA CHAKRA
THIRD EYE CHAKRA

VISHUDDHA CHAKRA
THROAT CHAKRA

ANAHATA CHAKRA
HEART CHAKRA

MANIPURA CHAKRA
SOLAR PLEXUS CHAKRA

SWADHISHTHANA CHAKRA
SACRAL CHAKRA

MULADHARA CHAKRA
ROOT CHAKRA

Engage with Your Observer

The tradition I was raised in told of a great war in heaven before Earth was created, where two brothers, Jesus and Lucifer, presented plans for Earth and humanity to their Heavenly Father. Jesus had a plan that everyone on Earth would have free agency to make their own decisions. Lucifer did not want humanity to experience that freedom. Lucifer's plan was for everyone to be under control with no free agency. Jesus won the war and, therefore, his plan for Earth was implemented and humanity was granted free will.

Wisdom traditions from around the world describe the same divine qualities in humanity, with one being freedom to choose. Free will, free agency, sovereignty over one's life—these are considered self-evident powers of humanity. There are many other stories, myths, and archetypes that present a similar message, all to emphasize the great power of our freedom to forge our own destiny, to create our own path, and to make our own decisions.

Clarity of mind is crucial for accessing this greatest power. In meditation, we practice cultivating observer consciousness, or seeing things as they really are. The observer is the witness, the soul, and the higher self, and it looks at things more objectively than our ego mind can. The observer also has a connection to and understanding of eternity that provides us with great wisdom and comfort in times of uncertainty or confusion. Recognizing and engaging our observer allows us to divorce ourselves from our ego and look at ourselves, our behaviors, and our actions *with* compassion and *without* judgment.

When we are in a good place, rested, and at peace with ourselves, it can be easy to hear the voice of the observer, the witness, or our higher selves. When the voice of the ego is loud, it's not easy to hear the voice of the observer. Here are a few ways to identify the voice of the observer:

- ▶ The observer delivers calm, rational, nonjudgmental thoughts and ideas. It takes time to respond and is never aggressive. Are your thoughts calm and mindful?

- ▶ The observer is characterized by a premise of unity. Consider the message your thoughts are telling you. Does it bring you closer to others and the world around you?

- ▶ The observer operates primarily from a place of compassion, even-mindedness, acceptance, and present-moment awareness. Does the voice you hear have any of these qualities in the undertone of its message to you?

DISIDENTIFYING WITH OUR EMOTIONS

Emotions can be extremely powerful, and in a heightened emotional state, our ego often takes control. We often say, "I am sad," or "I am worried," which mentally acts as an affirmation, creating more of the emotion we are experiencing.

One way we can allow our emotions to come and go more easily is by "noting" them, rather than identifying with them. Meditate today and observe the emotions you experience. Note them, rather than identify with them. Instead of saying, "I am sad," say, "There is sadness." Instead of saying, "I feel anxious," say, "There is anxiety." Even practice this with positive emotions; for example, if you are happy, say silently, "There is happiness."

TUNE IN TO YOUR HIGHER SELF

Think about the last time you acted on an unhealthy behavior or habit. There was a part of you that knew it was unhealthy, a part of you that could have stopped yourself from making that mistake, taking that extra bite, or saying those unloving words. Your higher self can be heard as the "still, small" voice within. The spiritual path is about listening to that higher voice.

In certain situations, the ego's voice has the most practical advice or support for you to accept. Imagine a situation where your spiritual inner voice says, "All is one, all is love, the person in front of you is lacking love," but your ego voice says, "This person is unwell and intends me harm." These are the situations the ego was made for.

In the past, we have looked at things on a spectrum from bad to good. Shakespeare beautifully articulated the reality of perception when he said, "There is nothing good or bad, but thinking makes it so." This is true about activities, medicine, and other experiences. Another great mind, Harry A. Overstreet, takes this concept in another direction, specifically in reference to personal behavior. In his book *The Mature Mind,* Overstreet presents a new perspective on personal behavioral development, where the "bad" to "good" spectrum is transformed into an "immature" to "mature" spectrum. This can be very helpful, not only because it's more sophisticated in its implications, but also because it removes the damning shame around our "badness."

A Serbian proverb says, "Be humble, for you are made of earth; be noble, for you are made of stars." Think about what this means for you. Deepen your personal connection to your own dual nature. It isn't that part of you is bad, but that a part of you is still learning. Never forget, however, there is a part of you that already knows. You have access to extraordinary wisdom within, and it is there for you, accessible at any time, only through the depth of your sincerity and willingness to use it.

Each of us must take full responsibility for our actions, and there's no way we could go over every detail of every possible scenario we could find ourselves in. So, rather than attempt to prepare yourself for *everything*, I advise you to be prepared for *anything*. Develop a relationship with your two sides and the two voices that they speak from. Learn how they can communicate with one another, compromise, negotiate, and come to an agreement. Some of the best ways to calm the ego are to relax, practice good self-care, and meditate.

Tune in to your higher self by cultivating a sense of the energetic quality of your higher self. Meditate on the characteristics of the higher self and the ego; get to know them intimately. You can even imagine an angel on your right shoulder and a devil on your left, like in cartoons, and begin to put a mental image to the tone, energy, and quality of each voice.

The ego will assassinate the character of someone with whom we have some kind of difficulty. The observer will accept things as they are and make needed recalibrations. The ego will puff you up with false pride and arrogance. The observer will give you courage and confidence. The ego will gossip, slander, and blacklist others. The observer will encourage forgiveness, amends, and well-wishes.

Choose to fall in love with who you really are. The ego finds fault but your higher self will help you develop a healthy sense of self-love, which will make self-care and spiritual development easier, more interesting, and more fun. Maturation is a good thing. There is a societal problem, a pervasive dysfunctional belief that maturity isn't fun or sexy. That is not true. Maturity means greater understanding, more experience, and a better deployment of that understanding and experience. Your higher self is the aspect of you that will guide you there, and every time you make a decision from your higher self, you increase its influence over your lower nature, thus gradually and naturally infusing your reality with greater spiritual potency and power.

UNDERSTANDING THE EGO AND THE HIGHER SELF

Here's a simple list for you to reflect on to help you understand the qualities of the ego and the higher self. If you're experiencing one or another, it's the result of your consciousness primarily operating out of the respective aspect of your nature.

EGO:

Anger	Dysfunction	Manipulation
Arrogance	Gossip	Violence
Bitterness	Greed	
Disconnection	Hatred	

HIGHER SELF:

Compassion	Flexibility	Order
Connection	Generosity	Peace
Encouragement	Happiness	
Faith	Joy	

TUNING IN TO YOUR HIGHEST SELF

The following exercise is designed to help you tune in to your higher self, calm the ego, see things from a bigger perspective, and create space between your truth and your thoughts and emotions.

TIME   30 TO 60 MINUTES

WHAT YOU'LL NEED

- ▶ Journal and a pen
- ▶ Comfortable place to meditate
- ▶ Timer

OPTIONAL

You may choose to increase the spiritual quality of this experience by adding elements like fresh flowers, white clothing, white candles, and other components that feel meaningful to you. You may also choose to practice this exercise at night right before bed to imprint your mind more potently or first thing in the morning to set the intention for your day.

GET STARTED

1. Set a timer for 10 to 40 minutes and lie flat on your back with your hands resting face down on the sides of your body. Place a pillow under your head, if you'd like.

2. Begin to meditate using the mantra *fiat veritas,* which means, "let truth be known" or "there is truth." This will help you tune in to your "true colors." Silently repeat *fiat* with every inhale and *veritas* on every exhale.

3. As always, allow the exhale to bring a wave of relaxation through every part of the body.

4. Observe the thoughts as they arise in your mind and note: *There is a thought about work.* Or, *There is a thought about Mom.* Observe emotions and feelings as they arise, but do not identify with them: *There is peace here.* Or, *There is sadness here.*

5. After noting a thought or feeling, come back to the breath and the mantra.

6. When the timer sounds, set it for 10 to 40 minutes more to begin the second half of your meditation.

7. You will now meditate using the mantra *ad lucem*, which means "on to enlightenment" or "toward the light." Breathing in, repeat a*d*; breathing out, repeat *lucem*.

8. For the duration of the meditation, pair your mantra with the visualization of yourself as the highest version of yourself: feeling connected to others, generous, flexible, compassionate, joyful, happy, peaceful, confident, faithful. Feel these qualities; don't just visualize them. Embody them.

WRAP UP

When your timer sounds, take a moment in silence, then write in your journal about the exercise, noting anything you felt throughout the process.

GO DEEPER

Revisit this practice when you feel disconnected from your higher self.

Live in Your Power

UNHEALTHY PATTERNS DON'T ALWAYS LOOK obviously unhealthy to us; they can mask themselves as freedom, personal expression, or having control over our experience. However, this is a trick of the ego—unhealthy patterns actually represent bondage to our lower nature and limitations in our divine expression. The ego would have you believe that captivity is freedom and ignorance is wisdom. This, of course, is untrue. To remain captive to our automatic behaviors is to passively surrender our free will and, therefore, relinquish our power. To remain ignorant to our shortcomings is to prevent ourselves from overcoming and moving beyond them.

As you learn and study more, your ego accompanies you on the journey. As we discussed in chapter 6, you must always anticipate your ego. As you grow, your ego will increase in its sophistication, so you must remain one step ahead at all times. Your ego will use the new information you learn to justify dysfunctional behavior in new ways. Dysfunctional behavior and dysfunctional thinking habits must be recognized for what they are in order to alchemize and transmute them into something healthy. Befriend your ego. Learn to laugh at its lies.

Don't be afraid of the lies the ego tells. Expect them. They will never go away, but your relationship with them can change. You can learn to recognize the ego's voice and strengthen your power to override it. Recognizing your shortcomings offers extraordinary freedom. It allows us to see things as they really are, to see ourselves as we really are. Our power is found not in delusion, ignorance, or bypassing, but, rather, in truth.

In this chapter, we will discuss the ways in which we can live from our genuine source of power and avoid the traps the ego lays. We will look at the power of setting intentions and cultivating gratitude to tune in to an empowered state of mind. And we'll revisit the necessity of letting go of that which does not serve us and how it helps us manifest our potential and demonstrate a new expression of ourselves in our lives and in the world.

SET INTENTIONS

Setting an intention means planting the seed of something you'd like to create or experience in your awareness. What does that actually mean? I have found it most powerful and effective to look at intention setting as a way to choose consciously to focus your energy in a specific direction.

Take some time to be clear on one big goal or dream you have and start thinking about the intentions you need to set to bring that goal or dream to life. Your goal can be as simple as establishing a habit of a regular fitness regimen or as complex as running for political office. Be open to alternate expressions of your dream and goal, trust the process, and start to imagine what it will look and feel like to fully realize that goal or dream. Never forget the metaphysical principle of the unity of all things and the law of karma. If your intention has any negative or harmful undertones to it, you can expect that your goal will not bring you fulfillment. Anything you send out will come back to you—and this includes hidden and passive harm.

When setting intentions, practice nonattachment to specific outcomes. Nonattachment means we will do our best in any given situation, while maintaining a healthy relationship to all possibilities. When we have a mental and emotional attachment to specific outcomes, we develop an unhealthy expectation—and expectations are rarely met, causing us drama, despair, and suffering. Conversely, nonattachment leaves room for multiple favorable outcomes and contributes to the cultivation of the attitude of the positive onlooker.

A daily meditation practice will help you develop the ability to detach from the thoughts, memories, or emotions processing in the psyche. The deeper you can relax in meditation, the more receptive your mind and body will be to the imprint of your intention. When we tune in to the observer state, we no longer judge, criticize, reminisce, or worry—we are completely present, observing things as they are in the moment. This state of pure awareness has a cleansing effect. Your own doubts, fears, and insecurities are silent. That's why it's an excellent time to set an intention.

Support your intention with curated thoughts, affirmations, smaller goals, and exercises to help you clear anything from your life that might prevent you from achieving what you want. You may also choose to journal about your intentions so you can become clearer about your specific goals and the aspects that are especially important to you. Use Future Moment Time Travel (see page 98) to deepen your connection to your goal.

Affirmation Myths and Truths

We all think tens of thousands of thoughts each day, many of which may feel out of our control. But we have the ability to curate those thoughts using affirmations. Strictly speaking, an affirmation is a statement that "affirms" that which is true. For our intents and purposes, there is more to an affirmation than just declaring something specific into existence. To understand truly how to develop powerful affirmations, we have to debunk some affirmation myths.

Myth #1: The most effective affirmations are specific and exclusive to your goal.

"I will exercise four times a week, every week, for the entire year."

Truth: Although you should set clear intentions and your affirmations should be in perfect resonance with those intentions, exclusivity can reinforce an unhealthy attachment to specific outcomes. Practice being inclusive to various expressions of a positive outcome by using inclusive affirmations.

"I will find new and exciting ways to incorporate exercise into my lifestyle."

Myth #2: Your positive affirmations should use declarative statements to speak to exactly what it is you want to have or experience.

"I am in the best shape of my life."

Truth: Although it is important to incorporate declarative statements, neuroscientific research shows you must also incorporate relevant questions so your unconscious mind will begin to seek answers. Don't let your affirmations feel like complete lies. Find a way to bridge the storyline from where you are to where you want to be.

"I am in great shape. What are the best ways for me to increase my fitness level?"

Myth #3: Your positive affirmations should be spoken in the present tense, as if they have already come to fruition.

"I am in excellent shape."

Truth: Although we want to call something into present moment reality, we also must bridge the gap from where we are to where we'd like to be. Practice using affirmations that have movement and momentum.

"I am dedicated to increasing my fitness level with every passing day."

FUTURE MOMENT TIME TRAVEL

Work backward from your goal using this time travel meditation technique. Imagine yourself in a future where you have fully realized a specific intention, in a way that no beings experienced any harm. In fact, to best partner with universal cosmic forces to make this dream a reality, set the intention that your dream will not only be harmless, but also bring benefit to all beings. Tune in as deeply as possible to a timeline where this has been achieved.

Now, observe the journey from where you are now to that future moment. What could it look like? Step backward from that future moment and consider the following:

- ▶ What had to happen for this dream to become fully realized?

- ▶ What changes did I have to make to become the person who could realize this dream?

- ▶ What changes can I make now so I can step on the timeline?

When reflecting on what will make your dream a reality, avoid things like lottery winnings, gifts, surprises, and windfalls. Be open to receiving these kinds of things if they happen to show up along the way, but let go of magical thinking and do not aim your intentions in that direction. Focus on making real change in your life so you can legitimately self-transform to demonstrate the manifestation of this dream.

Focus on Gratitude

When we are children, we are taught to "ask nicely" and say "the magic words: please and thank you." There is a deeper truth here. It's not about using false kindness to get what we want; rather, it's about living in a higher vibrational field of deep respect, genuine gratitude, and authentic kindness.

Practicing gratitude sends signals to the brain about what is good and what we want to create and experience more of. Anything we think about, we will begin to find more of in our lives—so gratitude is an important place to start. When we celebrate something, we express deep gratitude for it. That's why parties, feasts, and festivals exist, to allow a collective experience of gratitude to boost the energetic morale of a community, family, or group. Keep this in mind the next time you find yourself celebrating. What are we celebrating? What are we grateful for and, therefore, creating more of?

Negativity is disempowering. By contrast, appreciation is empowering. Anger, aggression, and even depression cannot be present in the same place as sincere gratitude. Appreciation is a profound affirmation of the goodness of one's being, and it is the key to accessing the power of the present.

Recall a time when someone expressed heartfelt appreciation for something you did or said. Take a moment and think about it. We often block ourselves from deeply receiving the expression of gratitude from others because of a sense of internalized self-criticism. So, not only should you take a moment now to *think* about a time or two when someone expressed genuine appreciation for you, but you should *feel* it and fully receive it, as if the gratitude is being expressed in the present moment. Do this by taking a few deep breaths, allowing the body to relax, and remembering as much as you can about that one moment when true thankfulness was offered to you. Practice presence, openness, and receptivity the next time you are offered gratitude. If you can effectively receive gratitude in the moment it is being offered, you will experience a surge of joy—and so will the individual offering it to you.

You might notice that when you allow yourself to be open to gratitude, a charge of almost supernatural energy washes over you. When someone appreciates us, it's as though they're holding a mirror to our highest self, the one we sometimes struggle to see. The appreciation offers us profound affirmation: You are lovable, worthy, acceptable, and cherished. In that moment, something about you is just perfect. When our worth is articulated and reflected through the eyes of another, our insecurities and worries about our worthiness are assuaged. The pressure to be perfect is lifted, because in at least some small way, we are being reminded we are already perfect.

From a metaphysical perspective, gratitude is the key to growth and expansion. Just as you experienced receiving gratitude, you will now learn to practice radiating gratitude to fill the world around you with that same surge of life force energy.

In the physical world, when we give something away, we lose it. If you give your friend a bouquet, you no longer have the flowers. In the metaphysical dimension, when we give something away, we receive more of it. If you offer genuine gratitude and service from a place of nonattachment to outcomes, you increase the vibrational frequency of that energetic quality and, therefore, experience more of it. Gratitude is the first step in working with this kind of metaphysical energy.

HAPPY AND GRATEFUL

Affirmations act as curated thoughts. Fill your mind with thoughts of gratitude by practicing gratitude affirmations:

I am so happy and grateful for my friends and family.

I am so happy and grateful for my sense of self.

I am so happy and grateful for my commitment to personal growth.

I am so happy and grateful for _____.

LET GO TO GET GOING

Gratitude is also an incredible resource while we work through uncomfortable situations and let go of that which no longer serves our well-being. Our thoughts fill our minds and those thoughts make up the pool of data from which we choose our words. Our words then affirm and strengthen those thoughts in our mind, while also communicating where we stand to the world around us. We begin to believe that which we have spoken to ourselves and others, and our actions follow suit. By embodying a sense of genuine gratitude for all the benefits and blessings that surround you, you will begin to train your mind to seek and find that which is good.

When we release what no longer serves our health and progress, it's important to name and acknowledge that which no longer works. It's as if we have to walk ourselves through the story line: "I was doing this behavior, which is actually not good for me. So, now, I am letting go of that behavior so I may move on to the next season of my life and learn new lessons."

Discussing our character defects, fears, shortcomings, or other things we need to overcome can be challenging, so practicing self-compassion is important. Although you should be as gentle and kind with yourself as possible, you should also allow yourself to experience genuine remorse. There is no way around learning the lesson your challenges have presented. You can delay the learning for as long as the ego is in control, but the higher self knows better.

When we make a mistake, the feelings of remorse and contrition can be powerful incentives for self-transformation and change. It's important to be patient with ourselves, and it's equally important to hold ourselves to a high standard and allow ourselves to experience these feelings, decreasing the chances of making the same kind of mistake again.

This is a balancing act. The ego will try to punish you for your mistakes with shame and guilt, and the ego will also try to justify the mistakes without taking responsibility for them. Do not allow your ego to control this process. Your higher self is always there; you just need to make the conscious decision to hand your challenges, weaknesses, shortcomings, pain, and shame over to the higher self to allow it to be purified. This purification involves disengaging with qualities that limit and harm to create space for the expression of qualities that better represent your highest nature.

MANIFEST YOUR POTENTIAL

Science has yet to come anywhere near quantifying the power of the human spirit and mind. You can overcome extraordinary adversity and manifest incredible creations—and this is all completely natural. The power to create and become something new is an aspect of the higher nature and it lies deep within as dormant potential, awaiting your conscious determined activation of it. It can be corrupted by the lower nature if it is used to cause harm, but the act of manifesting something new is an expression of our divine nature. In this section, we will discuss what it means to intentionally create experiences and demonstrate higher qualities to manifest your potential.

A few things to keep in mind: Letting go of unhealthy patterns is a gradual process, but you have the power to overcome any adversity that life presents. Even if you aren't already expressing greatness, remember, it is simply dormant inside you; it is not absent. Finally, remember to look at the lives of others for inspiration, but not comparison. Your journey is not theirs.

To manifest something is to take it from the realm of concept or idea and move it, through your actions, into physical expression. The important part here is to remember the body-mind connection. Breath control and conscious relaxation are two easy ways to begin to allow your conscious mind to move into the driver's seat of the body, allowing the higher nature of conscious intention to influence the lower nature of behavior.

As we discussed in chapter 4, manifestation works in concert with the Law of Attraction and Repulsion. To manifest an experience, we first demonstrate the relevant vibration and behaviors needed to become more magnetically attractive to it. Any professional actor will tell you that when they go into an audition desperately needing that role, the energy of desperation emphasizes the sense of lack and rarely (if ever) creates the desired result. An actor who goes into an audition in energetic harmony with the role, embodying it effectively and accurately, increases the likelihood of getting the job.

Worry, fear, and anxiety energetically emphasize the sense of lacking. They remind you and the world around you of what you *don't have*, what you *aren't already*, and what *isn't happening*. As we tune in to gratitude with love in our hearts, fear begins to fade, like turning on a light. Shadows do not have their own substance; rather, they are the lack of light. Fear is the lack of love; it isn't the presence of something else. Love and gratitude help us attune ourselves to the right conditions that will result in the manifestation of our potential.

A TOTALLY NEW EXPERIENCE

This exercise is designed to help you disengage from the momentum of old patterns and focus attention and energy onto a clear, powerful intention. It will also help you generate new momentum to achieve more of what you want to create and experience in life.

Keep in mind, these exercises are extremely powerful, so be patient with yourself and take your time to do them as accurately as possible.

TIME 30 TO 60 MINUTES

WHAT YOU'LL NEED

- ▶ Journal and a pen
- ▶ Timer

OPTIONAL

Consider this exercise somewhere between a sacred ceremony and a powerful consultation with yourself. Clean your environment as you prepare for this exercise. I also recommend doing this exercise in the morning so you can use it to build energetic momentum throughout your day.

Each meditation session should last between 5 and 20 minutes.

GET STARTED

1. Begin meditating. Close your eyes and bring awareness to the breath. Feel a real, deep sense of gratitude.

2. Silently ask yourself, "What do I want to experience?" Allow your body to be still until your mind provides a clear response to the question. Write down the response and return to meditating.

3. Write down any further responses as they come, one at a time, returning to meditating between each response. Continue until your timer sounds.

4. Look at what you've written and ask yourself, "Is this really what I want?" Cross out anything that doesn't feel connected to your deepest truth. Circle what stands out as something you'd like to manifest and read those items aloud.

5. Close your eyes and begin your second meditation. Let your exhales bring a sense of relief and relaxation throughout the body, opening your mind to seeing things differently.

6. Silently reflect on the desire(s) you circled and ask yourself, "How do I become the person who has this experience?" Allow your body to be still until your mind provides a clear response to the question. Write down the response and return to meditating. Write further responses as they come until your timer sounds.

7. Look at what you've written. Fill in the blanks with the behaviors you need to do to become this person: "I am willing to _____, _____, and _____ to become the person who has the experience of _____."

8. Begin your third meditation. Close your eyes and allow all the muscles in your body to soften. ➤

9. Silently ask yourself, "What are the faults or shortcomings preventing me from being in magnetic harmony with this experience?" Write down the blocks and limitations that come to mind.

10. Continue meditating on the same question, writing down what comes to mind until your timer sounds.

11. Reflect on what you've written and tell yourself, "I am able to overcome these blocks and limitations. I am open to doing what it takes to overcome these blocks and limitations. I am willing to change these behaviors and patterns to manifest the experience of _____. I am determined to see all these things differently and to conduct myself in a new way."

12. Begin your fourth meditation. Breathe comfortably and work consciously with the exhales, allowing them to settle the body just a little bit deeper into decompression.

13. Silently ask yourself, "What can I do today to make progress in increasing my vibrational resonance with this experience?" Write down the response that comes up. Stay in meditation until your timer sounds.

14. Stand up and stretch your body in any way that feels comfortable for you. Then, stand up straight with your hands on your hips and chest slightly out, in a power pose of confidence. With your eyes closed, take a few deep breaths.

15. Review the pages in your journal and write a four-part intention based on the information gathered in your meditations, following this structure.

- I will experience _____ in a way that benefits my spiritual growth and only benefits the lives of all those with whom I come in contact.

- I will _____, _____, and _____ to become the person who has the experience of _____.

- I will change the behaviors and patterns of _____ to manifest the experience of _____.

- Today I will _____ to make progress in increasing my vibrational resonance with the experience of _____.

16. Again, stand up, stretch, and put your hands on your hips in the power pose.

17. With your eyes closed, take a few deep breaths, maintaining your power pose. Read your four-part intention aloud, speaking with confidence, courage, and strength.

18. Read it again three or more times, seeing it in your mind and feeling it in your body, and speaking with honesty and sincerity in your voice.

WRAP UP

Do not rush out of the exercise without making a record of what you did. Journal about your experience, impressions, challenges, and insights that came up during this exercise. Move forward today taking direct action based on your intention. ➤

GO DEEPER

Take these intentions with you. Create reminders of them for yourself. Consider what you read, watch, listen to, or otherwise engage in and how these actions may help or harm your ability to manifest your potential. Make necessary changes. Create a playlist to specifically support the changes you are making to become the person who will experience that which you are manifesting; revisiting the Conscious Playlist (page 42) may help.

Discover Your Purpose

WHY AM I HERE? WHAT is my purpose? Humans have asked these questions since the beginning of time. From a metaphysical perspective, there is one foundational universal purpose that all living beings share: to love and grow. So, why doesn't this answer feel satisfactory?

Because of the highly individualized nature of each person's path, love and growth looks different to us all. There is no one other than you who can tell you what your life purpose is. But this chapter is intended to help you experience a process of self-discovery. Your purpose will take on the core qualities of love and growth, but it will look very different from any other person's life purpose. Those core qualities of love and growth will demonstrate themselves through any number of careers, relationships, and projects.

We will explore the necessity of being very present in finding your purpose. We'll also examine how your purpose is not a stationary assignment given to you from on high, but an ongoing, morphing sense of meaning that expresses itself through every situation and context. You will be encouraged to disengage from harmful, negative, inhibiting kinds of thinking and you will be given tools to help you deepen your connection to the inner guidance system that will lead you to a sense of fulfillment through purposeful love and intentional growth.

START TODAY

All your power exists right here, where you find yourself right now. When you reflect on finding your purpose, notice how the ego will project into the future. Instead, look at the world around you now. Take just one moment, glance up from this book, and scan your surroundings. Allow your gaze to take it all in as you observe your mind.

What came into your mind as you looked around? The present moment has extraordinary information and guidance for you. If you're at home, perhaps you noticed small chores you'd like to take care of; if you're out in public, perhaps you noticed things that need to change. Regardless of what it was, there are subtle clues to your purpose. If you're at home and you glanced around, maybe you noticed a gift you have to wrap, laundry that needs to be done, or a room that needs to be cleaned. Now, I get it—that may not seem to be a grandiose and powerful purpose for a holy, divine child of God. But what would happen if you did that chore?

As we've discussed, healthy behaviors give the body a sense of reward and accomplishment through a dopamine release. After a yoga practice, you have a sense of elation. After a self-care practice, you feel refreshed. After cleaning the whole house, you feel a sense of accomplishment. There are natural, healthy feelings of goodness and fulfillment that happen in moments following the simplest of tasks. From a spiritual perspective, there is a reason for that. These healthy doses of dopamine are indicators that we are on the right track, that we are doing things that contribute to our growth, and that we are moving in the right direction. Dysfunctional and addictive behaviors provide a counterfeit feeling of reward and accomplishment, whereas healthy behaviors provide the real thing.

The best way to find our purpose is to take action—right here, right now. Instead of overthinking whether we will be good at something, whether it will work out, or whether we should try it, observe the circumstances your life has provided. Imagine the universe conspiring to support you as you fulfill your purpose and know you have everything you need when you need it.

Take small steps toward your purpose by trying new things. Approach your circumstances with a new outlook. Revisit your current situation with new eyes and observe the results. Clarity of purpose often comes with consistent action, with attempts and failures, and with doing rather than thinking. Knowing how to work out does not create a fit body, but a long-term commitment to working out does. The same is true of other things. You never know until you try. The learning you experience along the way is a pivotal part of the process and the growth you undergo is your purpose.

5-5-5-5 BREATH

Conscious breathing has the ability to slow down an overactive mind and bring us deeper into the present moment. Practice 5-5-5-5 breath for five minutes.

1. Breathe in for five seconds.

2. Hold the breath for five seconds.

3. Breathe out for five seconds.

4. Hold the empty lungs for five seconds.

5. Repeat.

Go Toward What You Love

We've all heard the expression, "If you love what you do, you'll never work a day in your life." Find what you love doing. Think about the things you could do all day, the things that cause time to fly by. What do you look forward to? What makes you feel alive? By going toward what you love, you begin to unlock new levels of bliss, fulfillment, and wisdom. With wisdom comes greater enlightenment and understanding. Don't be afraid. Have faith that no matter what happens, things will work out. All of us will die one day, and even in that, everything is okay. I know this can be scary, painful, and unnerving sometimes, but always remember to breathe. Don't be afraid to slow down and take a few deep breaths to bring you into the present. Remember, the only constant in life is change, and the sooner we learn to embrace change, the more resilient we become.

There could be a spiritual clue hidden in the things you love. We often find that something we love becomes part of our dharma, or part of the unique magic that makes us who we are. When we love something, we embrace it, saturate ourselves in it, and understand it in a way others may not. Learn to recognize when your heart comes alive and observe what you love. Move toward it.

There are things in our lives we really don't love—and I'm not talking about budgeting your finances or doing the dishes. Just as certain things can make us come alive, other things can feel like a waste of time and energy. We need, either, to become more efficient about doing these things or move into a new phase of our lives so they no longer drain us of our precious energy and time.

Move toward creating a life full of the things you love, with fewer things that drain you of vitality and joy. Discovering your purpose is not a one-time decision or realization. It's an ongoing, ever-changing journey. Being present is the practice that will help you tune in to the energy dynamic that will give you the most energy and fulfillment.

Forget About "the One"

I remember my parents teaching me that anyone could be my soul mate, because what makes them my soul mate is our equal commitment to our connection. The same is true in our life purpose. Many of us struggle to find our purpose because we try to find "the one" thing we were meant to do. You may go through seasons and times of deep passionate connection to one calling, only to find it prepared you for a reinvention, transition, and a new season in the experience of another calling.

There isn't one thing that will bring you total fulfillment. True fulfillment can only come through a deep connection to the creator of the universe and knowing you are doing everything you can to walk in alignment with a greater plan. Practice reminding yourself that you are an eternal spiritual being having a temporary human experience, as French philosopher Pierre Teilhard de Chardin taught us. The human experience is an adventure in experimenting and evolving, of trial and error.

In the Buddhist tradition, there is a thousand-armed bodhisattva named Avalokiteshvara, and in each of her thousand hands, she holds a different tool. Each tool is used to deliver compassion into the world in a different way. Remember, a bodhisattva is an ordinary person who has experienced true compassion in their heart and begun the spiritual path. Avalokiteshvara symbolizes all the many different approaches we can take on the journey. What we do doesn't matter, but how we do it does.

YOUR ONE THOUSAND ARMS

Reflect on the thousand-armed bodhisattva who holds a different tool in each of her thousand hands. Consider for a moment that you hold many different tools and play many different roles in your life. Use the following questions as journal prompts:

➤ What are the different tools I use in my life?

➤ How can I use these tools to deliver compassion?

➤ What are the different roles I play in my life?

➤ How can I use these roles to offer compassion?

AVALOKITESHVARA

Connect Passion with Action

Bringing consciousness into our actions is how we establish enlightened behaviors. But we can't be so afraid of making mistakes that we don't act. Yes, we should prayerfully think through our decisions—but indecision is a detriment to action. And we must take action. Our ability to act for ourselves is the great divine gift and, therefore, what we do is of utmost importance. Action is what leads to healing, and because healing and growth are one in the same, action is what creates growth as well. It isn't enough to know you should clean, disinfect, and nurse a physical wound for it to heal; you must perform the actions of cleaning, disinfecting, and nursing the wound to facilitate the conditions for its healing. The knowledge alone is not enough—it must be applied.

I know all about the healing power of meditation, but I only benefit from it when I take time to practice meditation, putting what I know and have learned into practice.

Sometimes, just having the insight and inspiration to make a change can make us feel a release that indicates we have done what needs to be done. But the truth is, we've only begun. A new behavioral pattern needs to be introduced and enacted repeatedly. This seems simple enough, but why don't we do it? Why isn't it easier to take action?

Newton's first law of motion states that an object at rest tends to stay at rest, and an object in motion tends to stay in motion, unless acted upon by another force. We have to call forth from within ourselves the force that will move us from stagnation and build momentum for action. That force is our passion. Passion is the fire that energizes and moves us to take action. Passion has the power to override the operating system and take use to the next level in our experience.

We discover our true passion through exploration and trial and error. Take flight! See what comes up for you in different circumstances and situations. We have to connect the things we're passionate about with conscious and intentional action. Try new things and don't be afraid of being uncomfortable. Just because you dive into an experience doesn't mean you need to stay there forever or that your identity is changed. Stay firm in your faith, remember who you are, and allow yourself to grow.

We have to get out of our own way and stop overthinking what it is we're meant to do. Too often, we wait for the outside world to validate us or to direct us. Remember, you are the captain of your ship. You are the star of your movie. You are the powerful, free-willed being here on your journey. The more we experience, the more we learn about ourselves and our abilities.

Consider tumbled stones. They are smooth and shiny, and by their color and texture, you can see exactly what they are. However, these stones didn't begin that way. They had rough outer edges and were likely caked in other minerals and earth. They have to be cleaned and put through the tumbling process with other grist and chemicals to reveal their true state. Consider your experiences the grist that helps polish and smooth, revealing more and more about your unique nature. This process can connect us to our higher selves and give our lives deeper meaning.

LOVE IN ACTION

This exercise will bring your mind and body into alignment with a deeper sense of compassion and loving-kindness. You will practice seeing yourself, your circumstances, and the world around you as wholly lovable and train your mind to think about ways you can express compassion in action.

TIME   30 TO 60 MINUTES

WHAT YOU'LL NEED

▶ Journal and a pen
▶ Timer

OPTIONAL

This is a great exercise to make special by bringing in sacred elements, such as beautiful music, candles, or incense.

GET STARTED

1. Set your timer for 10 to 20 minutes, lie on your back, and begin with a self-healing meditation.

2. Spend the first few minutes in stillness, allowing the body to soften into deep relaxation.

3. Envision your body glowing with a warm light representing love, especially in your hands.

4. Cultivate a sense of loving-kindness. You may choose to think about people you love deeply to help you embody a deep sense of compassion.

5. Cup your hands and hold them against your body as you allow every exhale to send a wave of relaxation through your body.

6. Use your hands to send healing to each part of your body: the crown of your head, the front and back of your neck, down your torso, legs, and feet. Be open to receiving a deep sense of nourishment, healing, compassion, and acceptance from this.

7. When your timer sounds, set it for 10 to 20 minutes more, and sit upright.

8. Silently repeat the mantra *caritas acta*, which means "love in action" or "charity done."

9. When your timer sounds, scan your environment in a relaxed way and continue repeating the mantra.

10. Allow your gaze to rest on any particular objects that stand out to you and consider how you might use those objects to direct the light of your loving-kindness into the world around you. You do not need, literally, to take immediate action on your ideas. Just train your mind to see everything as a tool that can be used to deliver compassion to others.

11. You may also choose to walk around the room or throughout your home and pick up different objects you use every day, each time looking at the object, considering how it can be used to transmit goodness into the world, and whispering *caritas acta*.

➤

WRAP UP

Write in your journal about this exercise, especially any ideas that came to you about how you can support others through the various objects that surround you. Consider the premise of this exercise: that you need to be in a healthy state of self-compassion and acceptance to most effectively transmit those same qualities into the world.

GO DEEPER

As you move through your life, take this mantra with you wherever you go. Develop the habit of seeing things through the eyes of the compassionate action-taker.

Extend Acts of Service

WHEN WE WATCH A MOVIE, we learn about the characters as we watch them live their lives. We get glimpses of how they operate at home, when alone, as they walk through the streets of their city, and in subtle, quiet interactions with family members. We can see that if a character receives grand benefits for their generosity, this may be the intention and purpose behind their generosity. We can also see that if a character extends an act of service and never discusses or receives credit for it, their motivation may come from a deeper, or *higher,* place within themselves.

Envision every single moment of your life as if it were a scene in a movie. As an exercise, become very present with yourself and reflect on just the last 24 hours. What do you notice? What are some qualities you learn about yourself? Think about the topics of conversation you bring up, the way you guide interactions, and the way you co-create that which unfolds. Recall private moments when no one else was around. It is said that character is how we behave when no one is watching. What did you say or do with yourself? What were you trying to do?

There is a metaphysical concept referred to as the Akashic Records. The concept has many other names, but it is simple and universal: every action, every thought, every movement is stored in a record. Nothing goes unnoticed by the universe and everything has an effect on some level. I sometimes like to look at our lives as the role we play in the Akashic Theatre. Imagine there is an audience of trillions observing everything you do. How might they describe your character?

In this chapter, we will discuss the spiritual relevance of generosity, service, and community within the context of how we deploy and activate our free will. On the surface, these things seem apparent or obvious, but there are deeper implications we will consider. These deeper considerations and the practices herein will help you settle the spiritual principles of service and generosity into your unconscious mind, establishing the possibility for service to become a way of life, rather than just conscious decisions.

Give Without Demand

Just as we must practice nonattachment to specific outcomes as we set our intentions, we also must practice nonattachment to outcomes when exercising generosity. The principle is about how we want to show up—with generosity of spirit—rather than what will happen because of our generosity. John Bunyan, 17th-century English writer and preacher, is famously quoted as saying, "You have not really lived until you have done something for someone who can never repay you."

A teen girl walked into a convenience store to buy a snack. She waited in line behind a young family buying a few basic groceries. When the cashier totaled up the family's grocery bill, they realized that did not have the money to pay for them. The girl looked in her pocket and found she had more than enough to pay for her snack. As the young parents scrambled in their pockets for coins, the girl said, "You dropped this at the door," and handed them a $20 bill, covering the rest of their bill. She didn't see them again and she didn't tell anyone what happened, but that family had groceries for one more day.

We are in a world where philanthropic generosity gets your name inscribed in marble walls and buildings named for you. From a spiritual perspective, these things are irrelevant and actually corrupt you. From a karmic perspective, when we are motivated by outward accolades and credit, that is the reward—and thus no real merit or good karma is actually generated. As we receive these false rewards of attention and credit, we begin to realize how temporary the reward of accolades really is, and a cycle of insincere generosity for the sake of personal branding or outward credit begins. Spiritually, this is a materialistic expression that leads to shallow generosity and meaningless attention seeking. To avoid the ego's trap, practice generosity in a way that does not draw attention to yourself. If you have a lot, give a lot. If you have a little, give a little, holding the desire to give more one day. Giving without demand for any kind of accolades or credit is a critical part of building a dedicated spiritual practice, as described through the universal cosmic law of consecration.

To consecrate something is to identify it as sacred. Consecrated oil has been blessed and is to be used only in a spiritual context, not for everyday purposes. To declare that all things are consecrated, as in the law of consecration, we indicate that the lower nature's opinion of ownership is mythological, just as our sense of separation is illusory. The law of consecration operates on the foundational principle that all is one and, therefore, everything belongs to all of us and no one should ever be without. This law is demonstrated in part through the many spiritual traditions and offerings that members of different communities make to ensure everyone has their needs met.

Sometimes I like to think of it like a mix-and-match game. Consider that everything you have is not really yours, but only temporarily in your possession to use to bless the lives of others. Look at all you have—your finances, your home, other possessions. Reflect on those with whom you come in contact. If they need anything in your possession, consider how you may be generous with them.

In certain seasons of our lives, we have more to give than in others. One thing that everyone can give, no matter their financial or material situation, is blessings over someone's life. A blessing is an expression of love born of the higher nature and based in truth. A blessing blesses the lives of the blessed, the one who offers the blessing, and all who come in contact with either party. Say encouraging, loving things to others. Every word you speak echoes in the minds of those within the sound of your voice, consciously or unconsciously, including you. When you lie, gossip, or attack, you speak curses out into the world, distorting the perception of reality. A curse is an expression meant to limit or block someone. Curses are born of the lower nature and based in lies. They cause harm not only to your target but also to you, as well as innocent bystanders. In different moments of our lives, we are the targets of these curses, their speakers, and the innocent bystanders. The farther you make it along the spiritual path, the less frequently curses will be part of your life. You will learn to use the gift of the tongue to bless.

Give generously of your word, with no expectation of recip-rocation. Allow your words of encouragement to be met with deep sincerity and they will often line up with actions that will provide genuine service to others. In what areas of your life are you already doing this? In what areas of your life can you do this more?

SERVE SELFLESSLY

Cultivate your ability to see things as they really are and you will begin to know, intuitively, how to be of service. There are no accidents, so where you are now is the perfect opportunity to begin to serve others. Who do you interact with on a regular basis? In what ways can you serve and bless them? Asking questions like these will send your brain on a quest to consider how you can help or support others based on your resources, gifts, and talents. It will also begin to lay the groundwork for establishing functional habits of service, which is the goal.

When committing to a practice of service, it is important to focus on the person you are serving. It's not about you or what you want to do. It's about them—what they need and what you can do to help meet that need. What will make a real difference for this person?

A mentor taught me about healing grief. He helped me process and learn from the suicide of one of my closest friends. I learned a lot about service in that experience, including that service comes in many more forms than I realized. Growing up, service meant mowing someone's lawn without charge or cleaning up the church building. As I grew, I came to learn that when someone is grieving, service can look like taking out the trash without being asked or leaving groceries on someone's doorstep. Other times, service looks like listening quietly while someone speaks about their heartbreak and pain.

Although we can work to establish an attitude of service and habits of service, service ultimately requires a decision to be there for someone else in a way that might provide them some benefit—big or small. We've heard the expression, "It's the thought that counts," and in some situations, that's exactly right. Doing the dishes for a friend, making a meal, or providing a few moments of attentive listening may not, in themselves, seem like big deals, but they can make quite a difference, especially when someone is in pain or feeling lost.

I AM YOU

The concept of reincarnation is considered an "exoteric" teaching, meaning it was taught to the public practitioners of numerous Eastern traditions in ancient times. However, the "esoteric"—meaning private, hidden, or inner—teachings of reincarnation revealed only to the highest initiates, are quite different from the idea of an ego identity dying and being reborn into a new body with a new set of circumstances. The esoteric teaching of reincarnation resonates more deeply with the metaphysical truth that all is one. The esoteric wisdom teaches that all spirits come from one great source. The teaching is intended to deepen our connection to each other's life so real compassion and empathy may be felt and spiritual love may be experienced.

Consider the people in your life and how you might serve them. Imagine in meditation that they are not simply other people, but you in another life. Imagine your mother, your brother, your friend . . . are all you in a past life. Breathe and let go of any judgments against them. See yourself in them. Notice what comes up and whether what you feel about them changes. This will help you love them more deeply and serve them with greater wisdom and sincerity.

APPRECIATE YOUR AGENCY

One of humanity's most divine characteristics is the principle of free agency or free will. Our ability to lead and guide our own destiny is an echo of the creative force that builds and creates all aspects of the universe. Think back to the tales of the Greek gods and goddesses. I remember learning about the fights and drama these gods and goddesses got into and I always found that fascinating—and a little confusing. If they were gods, wouldn't they be on the same team?

In chapter 5, we emphasized the spiritual principle of our divine nature, that as children of the creator of the universe, we have a destiny to become more like our divine source. Free agency is what gives us the opportunity to express whether we are wise or unwise divine children, just as the gods and goddesses of Greek scripture revealed a variety of characteristics, which did not always include wisdom.

Reflect on the decisions you make. Sure, some are better than others, but when you really have a chance to ponder and consider all outcomes, you tend to make a better decision. This is why meditation is so crucial. Correctly practicing meditation will strengthen your prefrontal cortex, which rules decision-making, discipline, and intentional behavior. The actual exercise of meditation technique is not about achieving altered states of consciousness; it is about training the mind in discipline and strengthening your ability to make conscious decisions, rather than being led by the default habitual patterns of the lower nature.

Remember, as you establish healthy habits, you upgrade the lower nature, taming and training it to serve your higher nature. This is how we spiritualize our material nature. One of the most crucial expressions of our free will is in how we interrupt dysfunctional patterns. The next step is establishing functional patterns, the highest of which is a pattern of service to others. Becoming more advanced spiritually is not about the ability to pontificate or perform with a spiritual aesthetic. Rather, it is about one's ability to contribute effectively to the alleviation of suffering from other living beings.

CONTRIBUTE TO YOUR COMMUNITY

It's easy to be swept up in the demands of daily life. But establishing and honoring a sense of community, and recognizing one's place in it, can be fundamental in living a more purposeful, spiritual, service-driven life.

In my 20s, I worked in Hollywood as a celebrity publicist. I was hosting red carpet events, so my community consisted of celebrities, photographers, reporters, club promoters, models, and talent agents. When I needed something for an event, I knew whom to call, and my community was always there for me. However, when I was sick, I found I didn't have anyone to call. When I was depressed or lonely, my community didn't know how to be there for me. After a devastating loss, I knew I needed a community that could support the greater challenges life may bring, and so I began a professional transition. When I began phasing out of that career into a new one, I found that my community changed dramatically.

In my old community, our shared connection was the parties I threw. When I stopped having parties and began teaching meditation, everyone in my life changed almost overnight. The people who surrounded me were health-conscious and spiritually focused. Communities come in many shapes and forms. The universal values that matter most in a community are support for one another, the bearing of each other's burdens, and connection based on trust. What communities are you part of? What connections are they based on? In what ways are you there for members of your community? In what ways are they there for you?

Buckminster Fuller was a 20th-century inventor whose focus was making a more unified, functional world that distributed resources to everyone efficiently. He proposed a new kind of structure for buildings—a hemisphere made of interlocking lattice grids, which he called geodesic domes. When pressure is applied to one aspect of the dome, it is distributed evenly throughout the rest of structure, making the domes unusually strong.

This same principal finds expression in community life, too. When we look at our connections to one another in a community, as we bear one another's burdens, they become lighter. If a family member is in distress, a strong family will be able to ease the discomfort and challenge of the situation through direct support. It is said that it takes a village to raise a child, and this is extraordinarily true. Anyone raising a child can testify that the support of a community is crucial in distributing the many challenging tasks associated with it. All this comes together to demonstrate the necessity of being there for each other.

Because of the metaphysical principle of unity consciousness, we can recognize that helping one another is really helping ourselves. From a spiritual perspective, serving another person is also serving God and generates positive karma.

The path of spiritual development requires an active decision to contribute positively to others' lives. In ancient times, we needed individuals to separate themselves, to go off into the mountains and meditate to receive divine downloads, then provide the community with insight and wisdom. In modern spirituality, though the occasional retreat can be profoundly rejuvenating, the emphasis is on proactively providing relief for those within our reach and spiritualizing the activities of daily life.

ACTIVATING YOUR POWER

This exercise will help you tune in to your eternal higher nature and open your mind to seeing the world through that nature. You will work to disengage from the flighty level of thoughts and make these thoughts real through action.

TIME   30 TO 60 MINUTES

WHAT YOU'LL NEED

- ▶ Journal and a pen
- ▶ Timer

OPTIONAL

This exercise begins and ends with an intention that can be spoken aloud where you are or while gazing directly into a mirror. As always, you may choose to incorporate sacred elements to deepen your connection to the experience and activate your senses.

GET STARTED

1. Set an intention by saying aloud, "I dedicate this time to deepening my spiritual practice and commit to infusing every moment of every day with the presence of my higher self."

2. Sit upright in a comfortable position, set a timer for 10 to 20 minutes, and begin to meditate.

3. Visualize your spirit within as a wise, powerful, immortal angel. Imagine that this powerful angel has been sent to this planet in this specific body, at this exact time, to provide healing, generosity, and service to others.

4. Imagine this spirit's strength, power, and wisdom imprinting on you. Feel its divine assignment to provide healing, generosity, and service to others.

5. Imagine infusing all your day-to-day activities with the conscious awareness of your spiritual nature.

6. Imagine infusing all your day-to-day activities with the conscious awareness of your spiritual nature. Breathe deeply and calmly, holding the visualization until the timer sounds.

7. Open your journal to a clean page and write the following question at the top of the page: "How can I bring conscious service into my home, my relationships, my community, and the world at large?"

8. Consider this question as you begin your next meditation. Set aside your journal, set a timer for 10 to 20 minutes, and return to meditation.

9. Meditate using the mantra *acta*, *non idea*, which means "actions, not ideas."

10. Allow the body to become very relaxed and still as you meditate. Observe the images and thoughts that arise in your mind and return to the mantra. Continue until the timer sounds.

➤

11. Set your timer for 10 minutes more and begin writing in your journal, answering the question you wrote at the top of the page. Focus on writing specific actions you can take that will result in tangible benefits for other people who cannot reward or pay you in any way.

12. When your timer sounds, set an intention for yourself to take genuine action on some of the things you've written. Commit to being of real service to others as soon and as often as possible.

WRAP UP

Open your journal and give yourself some time to describe and memorialize this experience. The more you can describe what came to you in meditation, the more your brain will commit it to memory.

GO DEEPER

The deeper you go into this exercise, the more you will get out of it. Incorporate this consciousness into your normal day-to-day activities. Take out your calendar, planner, and alarm. Plan your upcoming days with more detail and set alarms to keep yourself on track. Name the alarms things such as "Mindful Breakfast" instead of just "Time for Breakfast." If you have to go to work, set an alarm for the time you should leave for work and instead of "Commute," name the alarm, "Mindful Driving Commute."

Practice Compassion

WHEN THE TOPIC OF COMPASSION comes up, we often think of a delicate, sentimental feeling of tenderness. However, the compassion we will review in this chapter has a deeper, more metaphysical message at its core. The highest metaphysical truth is that of the unity of all that is. This is the source of the compassion addressed here. Imagine seeing a wounded deer limping away from a car accident with a broken leg. Your heart aches with compassion for the pain it must be in, knowing that without human intervention, it may not have long to live. This compassion arises from a sense of sympathy for the deer. However, a deeper compassion would be a sense of empathy for the deer. Sympathy is being able to recognize that another being is in suffering; empathy is feeling that suffering along with it. Empathy is where we find the compassion of unity consciousness.

There is extraordinary power in recognizing our connection to one another and the service, generosity, and compassion that arises from that recognition. This idea is the opposite of the normal worldview that we are separate and, therefore, in competition with one another. Through disciplined self-observation and sincere practice, we can begin to experience glimpses of realization and shimmers of enlightenment where the truth of unity consciousness is gradually revealed. There is a multi-dimensional awareness wherein we can hold multiple perspectives at once, and *that* is what unity consciousness is. It is based on the truth that *all is one*, and unity consciousness itself is the awareness, realization, and experience of that oneness. Imagine a cell in the body living its life, believing it to be separate from all other cells, but suddenly realizing it is not just a cell, but one small part of a much larger, crucial whole. Each of us is one small part of a much larger, very important, whole; and though small, each of us is very important and powerful, individually.

Power comes into play when action is taken from that realization. Our spiritual path is about applying what we learn in the world around us and, little by little, demonstrating that we understand. In the principle of unity consciousness, you will also realize that you are just as deserving of compassion as anyone else; that, too, must be demonstrated through your actions and decisions.

EXCHANGE YOURSELF FOR THE OTHER

The momentum of day-to-day living can easily prevent us from slowing down, processing, and fully experiencing what we're going through. This is one reason Buddhist practice of *metta*, or loving-kindness, is so crucial for the modern spiritual practitioner—it places equal focus on receiving and giving loving-kindness. The deeper we feel and receive sincere love and acceptance for ourselves, the more authentic and rich the love we extend to others will be. This isn't about shallow selfishness, but a deep recognition of the interconnectedness of all things, as well as the value of each and every soul.

The Buddhist concept of exchanging oneself with the other provides a way of thinking that supports us in gaining greater perspective. We don't know what we don't know. Every person we encounter has something to teach us and we can quicken that learning through open-mindedness and the conscious practice of compassion. Tuning in to the experience of another person can help us serve others as though they were us, enrich and expand the way we see the world, and deepen our understanding of our personal pain. To see things through our eyes alone is to see the world one-dimensionally. To begin to see things through the eyes of many different people from different backgrounds and circumstances provides a multi-dimensional perspective.

Establishing a multifaceted perspective by consciously practicing loving-kindness helps us see things as they really are, rather than attempting to filter the world through our direct experiences. That's enlightenment—to see things as they really, truly are. Enlightenment goes by many names: Christ Consciousness, Buddha Consciousness, Krishna Consciousness, truth, cosmic consciousness, salvation, beatification, and others. What it comes down to is the complete perception of absolute truth, which also means the absence of glamour, illusion, or distortion of thought or perspective.

I once led a group of about 80 people on a healing retreat in Costa Rica. It was an incredible experience full of meditation, yoga, massages, healthy food, and shamanic ceremonies for healing and spiritual revelation. I've led several retreats like this, and each has been meaningful. One particular night, each of us told the shaman what our intention would be for that night's ceremony. The room was dark, lit only by a few candles. It smelled of copal incense, and the sounds of the Costa Rican wildlife echoed while the shamans sang and played their indigenous instruments.

I had written this elaborate intention to *do this* and *become that* . . . but when I found myself standing there, with the shaman, he asked, "Brother, what does your spirit seek?" In that instant, the intention I had written became irrelevant and the words that automatically poured out of my mouth were, "Christ Consciousness." He kissed my forehead and said, "Bless you, Ben Decker. Now go sit." Everyone was focusing on themselves. Some people were journaling, some stretching, others meditating, and a few even sleeping. I sat down and began to meditate.

At some point in the ceremony, I felt the presence of my ancestors. They said things to me like, "We knew this time would come," "We're proud of you," and, "Are you ready?" I felt my body soften and become weak as a rush of energy moved through me. I turned to lie on my side, and from deep within me came a presence. I opened my eyes, gazed around the room, and was filled with a love beyond any I had ever experienced. It was as though I could feel all the pain, uncertainty, heartbreak, joy, hope, and love that everyone in the room was experiencing in their lives. The presence within me felt familiar and so I asked, "Who is here?" The voice of Jesus Christ responded from within, "Little brother, you know it is me. You invited me here. I am here to give you a great gift, that you may see the world as I do. You are feeling my heart and seeing through my eyes."

When the ceremony was over, I did my best to take with me the love for others I felt during that supernatural encounter. I remembered the pain and sadness I saw in a friend who otherwise seemed happy and successful. I could list a thousand things I learned. But what it came down to was this: There is much more than meets the eye. My heart had been broken open, and a new dimension of compassion had been initiated. It changed my relationships, including my relationship with myself.

We don't need some big divine intervention to cultivate loving-kindness and see others as ourselves. In some ways, this is really about getting back to basics. We have to begin to realize that, in this big wonderful world, all those who surround us are worthy of great love and compassion—and yes, so are we. As we practice loving-kindness and seeing ourselves in another's point of view with nonjudgment, we deepen our personal connection to the collective psyche. We understand why we do the things we do, and grasp the reality that we are only as good as our psychological programming.

The expansion of our perspective helps us recognize that "the present moment" is not just in "the present location." Our compassion must extend beyond ourselves, beyond our households, beyond our neighborhoods and communities, beyond our side of town, and beyond our nation. Metaphysical compassion is about exchanging ourselves for the other—*every* other—and seeing just how small this world really is. Because once we understand that, we understand our incredible power to influence it for the better.

HEART OPENER

In yoga, there are two postures often paired together—the cat and the cow. These are great for warming up the body, awakening the spine, and opening the heart. Practice this exercise for about five minutes.

1. Get down on your hands and knees, with your back parallel to the ground.

2. Breathe in as you turn your head up, broaden your shoulders, and curl your spine down toward the ground for cow pose.

3. Exhale as you turn your head down and round your back upward toward the ceiling for cat pose.

4. Let your body rock to the left and right, front and back, and even rotate in circles—loosen up.

5. With every inhale, curl up, facing toward the sky for cow pose.

6. With every exhale, round your spine, tucking your chin in for cat pose.

CAT AND COW YOGA POSTURES.

Demonstrate Loving-Kindness

Traditionally, the metta meditation practice consists of three parts: offering oneself loving-kindness, extending loving-kindness to those whom we easily love, and offering loving-kindness to those for whom we have neutral feelings. Then, we must do the challenging thing: cultivate feelings of loving-kindness toward those with whom we have the most difficulty.

Finally, loving-kindness is delivered to the entire world and all beings throughout the cosmos. Visualize love radiating from the heart of God, the great cosmic source of all love, and streaming forth into the hearts of all living beings, across the planet, and throughout the world. Imagine that every planet and every star is a living being as well, being blessed with this transmission of loving-kindness. Envision that love calling all things into divine order, recalibrating, healing, nourishing, and bringing wholeness and peace into every situation, every circumstance, and every heart that lives. Breathe into it. Experience it. Receive it as you give it.

This is a powerful exercise that has been scientifically proven to change the structure of the brain in beneficial ways with extended practice. Although the practitioner may receive emotional and physiological benefits from the practice, the spiritual work is about demonstrating that loving-kindness in the world.

Consider the relationship between *manifesting* something and *demonstrating* something. To *manifest* something is to bring it out from the level of thought into the level of form, but to *demonstrate* something is to express it through our way of being and interacting with the world. The demonstration of the quality of loving-kindness builds the momentum with which we experience the things we'd like to manifest.

No matter what it is—health, wealth, better relationships—it comes in its purest form through the recognition of our inseparability from the world around us. These things can certainly be made manifest through manipulation, but when we do that, we face the karmic consequences. That which we release into the world must inevitably be returned and processed through our own direct experience, whether in this life or the next. We must do more than practice loving-kindness meditations; we must demonstrate loving-kindness. We must manifest a world where the loving-kindness of righteous hearts can be made tangible, can be felt and deeply experienced.

Offering love—to ourselves and others—acts as an antidote to hate, disconnection, and aversion. When we love something, we reach out and embrace it. When we are afraid or averse to something, we recoil and withdraw. Love unlocks the power to understand that which eludes us. When we look to those of different political beliefs or of different social opinions than us, what is the spiritually correct way to engage? Is it to bulldoze those you disagree with, using projection and blame? Is it to submit fully and surrender your own perspective? Neither will do. The loving-kindness must be received as it is given, and communication must happen from an openness to learn, simultaneously infused with a willingness to teach.

Consider the stories we tell ourselves and the profound impact they have on the world. Those around us tell themselves their own stories. Demonstrating loving-kindness means taking that loving-kindness practice into our real lives—off the meditation cushion and into our relationships and interactions, especially with those we have the most difficulty. Recall the basic principles of neural plasticity presented in chapter 2. It is possible to retrain how we feel about one another and allow that change to expand from beyond our personal experience into the collective. Wars will become a thing of distant memory, and even legend, when a critical mass of humanity has effectively demonstrated loving-kindness.

PRACTICAL TELEPATHY

Applying the principles of unity consciousness and the interconnectedness of all things, consider there is no such thing as a "private thought"–that on some level, every living being hears every thought every other person thinks.

In this variation on a loving-kindness meditation, imagine sending the following positive thoughts into the minds of every living person in the world:

"May all of us have all we need.

May all of us be loved in ways that are just right.

May all of us know what to do next in our lives.

May all of us be forgiven of our faults and shortcomings.

May all of us be healed in every possible way."

STAY OPEN TO VULNERABILITY

Exercising lofty meditation goals like loving everyone and everything can and *should be* challenging. The easier it feels, the more likely you aren't really going that deep or allowing yourself to really feel what's inside you. I'm not suggesting that loving-kindness practices should be uncomfortable or unpleasant. But I do want to suggest tuning in to your deeper strength and resilience and allowing your emotional capacity to be stretched. Compassion is inextricably linked to empathy and vulnerability.

As we exercise loving-kindness, practice exchanging ourselves for the other, and open our minds to seeing things differently, our empathic powers become more active. Tune in to your strength and avoid the all-too-common temptation to withdraw from others. Deepening our compassion for others can enable us to feel safe in our own vulnerability.

To be vulnerable is to let down your guard, disengage from tension and resistance, and surrender into openness. That act of surrender can be incredibly challenging, especially if we are holding on to shame, guilt, or insecurity. Our spirit longs to be loved and seen, but these things can never happen without vulnerability. No one has it all. No one is perfect. And that's what makes us all perfect. We are perfectly in our own process, morphing from one state to the next.

In meditation, as we deepen our power to engage our inner observer, we naturally begin to see our story from a more objective vantage point. In stillness, your spiritual nature has more freedom to move. Allow some time and space for your chi, your prana, your energy, your light, your spirit, whatever you want to call it; it knows what to do, but you have to let go and allow it.

You'll notice as you meditate that there will be times when uncomfortable thoughts and memories arise. Welcome them! Breathe through them. Let the energy they hold move through you so you can move to the other side of it. Surrender is not about weakness or exposing yourself to danger; it's about recognizing the infinite supply of power within. As you let go of pretense, your authenticity will shine through. And those painful things you went through, those traumatic memories you hate to think about, those weaknesses and insecurities you hide from the world, all become raw power at your disposal. All things are made new in the light of truth.

Vulnerability is about total honesty, and that begins with ourselves. Meditation can be the opportunity to enter a safe zone where we allow ourselves to surrender to the truth, accept ourselves as we really are, and allow shame and embarrassment to be alchemized into integrity and confidence. Learning to be honest and vulnerable with ourselves will help fabricate our different layers into integrity with one another, when we can begin to live in deeper integrity in our relationships. There is no power in who you'd *like to be*. All of your power is in who you *really are*.

See First with Your Soul

Befriending our dual nature entails recognizing that our higher nature has a larger perspective than our lower nature and that our lower nature requires patience and diligence to tame. Meditation is about allowing the lower nature to become more receptive to the imprint and conditioning the higher nature to allow evolutionary potential to express through us into the world.

Too often, the lower nature will trip us, leading us to justify, rationalize, or bypass the sometimes-challenging inner spiritual work. A friend and I were discussing the power of loving-kindness work and its ability to attune the lower nature to the ways of the higher nature. She began by sharing about her most vicious abuser, whom she successfully forgave and released through the metta loving-kindness practice. A mutual friend entered the conversation, and he had irritated her in a few ways, with a social faux pas or two, but nothing serious. I jokingly said, "May he be happy, may he be healthy, may he be free from . . ." and she interrupted me. "No. Not him. Basically everyone in the world but him." She laughed and was not serious, but the truth of the challenge to love and accept "even him" was apparent.

Sometimes, it can be easier to forgive someone of blatant offenses than to open our hearts to those who just rub us the wrong way. Practicing compassion helps us cultivate a familiar sense of what it feels like to operate from the level of our soul. An increase in intuition comes with the practice of true compassion because of our fundamental unity. Compassion is not about cutting ourselves down so another may benefit; compassion is recognizing that, through the eye of the soul, there is no separation between our needs and those of every other being.

METTA LOVING–KINDNESS MEDITATION

The power of a precisely practiced loving-kindness meditation is rooted in the notion that every living being deserves three things: happiness, peace, and freedom from suffering. The simplicity of this variation on a traditional metta, or loving-kindness, meditation is intended to support its depth. When there are fewer elements to think about, you may be able to go deeper into each one.

TIME   20 TO 40 MINUTES

WHAT YOU'LL NEED

- Journal and a pen
- Comfortable place to sit where you won't be interrupted
- Timer

OPTIONAL

You may choose to make this meditation special by showering beforehand, playing beautiful music, lighting candles, or wearing all white to symbolize purity. You may also display photos of those you love most to support the feeling of loving-kindness.

GET STARTED

1. Get into a comfortable position to meditate and set a timer for 20 to 40 minutes.

2. Begin your meditation by taking a few deep breaths and allowing your body to relax into the silent words you will speak.

3. Cultivate an inner sense of loving-kindness for yourself, silently saying, "May I be happy. May I be at peace. May I be free from suffering." Allow these words to sink in and become real for you.

4. Now, call to mind those who have cared for you deeply, your closest loved ones. Imagine them as happy as could be and feel compassion for their sadness and pain. Silently say to them, "May you be happy. May you be at peace. May you be free from suffering."

5. Next, envision those individuals you have neutral feelings toward, like the people you see in passing at the market. Offer them loving-kindness and say to them, "May you be happy. May you be at peace. May you be free from suffering."

6. Now, bring to mind those with whom you have the most difficulty. Realize that their negative attributes are, either, a matter of perception on your end or a result of deep suffering. Send them loving-kindness as well, saying, "May you be happy. May you be at peace. May you be free from suffering." Repeat as needed so you really feel the metta.

7. Finally, expand your sense of loving-kindness to all people across the globe. Notice what images come to mind and do your best to imagine people from all

➤

walks of life and cultures. Include all animals, plants, and the planet itself. Say, "May you be happy. May you be at peace. May you be free from suffering." Allow that message to echo into the cosmos into eternity.

8. Return your attention to yourself, silently repeating, "May I be happy. May I be at peace. May I be free from suffering." Continue meditating on loving-kindness until your timer sounds.

WRAP UP

Journal about the exercise, the different elements you added, the time of day you practiced, and anything you felt throughout the process. What specific thoughts came to mind about specific people? Did you experience a shift in perspective or have a particular memory?

GO DEEPER

Practice a loving-kindness walking meditation. As you walk around your neighborhood or a local park, send the loving-kindness mantra to everyone and everything you see: "May you be happy. May you be at peace. May you be free from suffering." Consider that every time you walk, you can turn your experience into a meditation, and every time you see another person, you can make your interaction with them a loving-kindness meditation.

11

Embrace the Art of Healing

DURING MAY, WHICH IS MENTAL Health Awareness Month, I planned to do daily live-streamed interviews with different experts, authors, and entrepreneurs on the topic of cultivating mental wellness. Day after day, my videos were going off without a hitch. The conversations were great, everything happened right on time, and the videos were being received well. I was doing yoga, meditating, praying, journaling, eating right, and life was on track, too. It was glorious. Then, an incredible moment I had been anticipating for weeks came up—my interview with Marianne Williamson!

Marianne had been a mentor and friend for several years, and it meant so much to me that she was opening her busy schedule to support my project. She was to be my featured guest, and I couldn't wait for our conversation. We started right on time, there were no technical difficulties, and it felt like we clicked immediately. She even texted me afterward and told me I was great—I was beaming with joy and gratitude.

Then something strange happened. My account was hacked, and that video file was deleted. Sure, there was a large live audience, but I wouldn't be able to edit the video into smaller clips to share in an ongoing way. In a nanosecond, I went from an enlightened joyful being to feeling pretty angry and frustrated with myself. There was nothing I could do, though. I had to accept that my expectations for the footage would not be met. Disappointed, I moved on, grateful that the video was live and that I had that moment to connect with Marianne. In the grand scheme of things, this wasn't a big deal. In fact, in the grand scheme of things, it was still a great experience I am very thankful for. I had to practice what I preach—I had to navigate it all with grace and resilience.

Even in the most challenging times, there is a way to move through the process with grace. Life carries with it disappointments, frustrations, and grief, even well into the journey of spiritual development. There really is an art to healing gracefully—and it is not always pretty. The practice of nonattachment allows us to be more nimble, more resilient, and quicker on our feet. As Marianne Williamson often says, "In life, it's not so much about what happens to us, as much as it is about who we are in the space of what happens to us." In this chapter, you will find tools and reflections to support you as you consciously and intentionally create a legacy, hold space for setbacks, and embrace the art of healing.

CREATE YOUR LEGACY

The beauty of life comes, in part, from its temporary nature. Death is also the ego's greatest fear. An aspect of spiritual maturation is recognizing that, one day, you will not walk the Earth and that you will leave a legacy made up of the lives you touched and things you created. Incorporating this recognition of the simple fact of your eventual death into your spiritual practice is not only connected to an ancient practice of impermanence, but also a way to ease your ego's concerns about death.

As time goes on, death becomes more and more familiar as our friends and loved ones pass away, moving on to the other side of the veil. From the world's perspective, death is the ultimate end. From a spiritual perspective, death is a powerful initiation into the next season in one's spiritual evolution. There's nothing morbid about living in such a way that you will leave behind a legacy worthy of your goodness. But it isn't about naming libraries for yourself or building statues in your likeness. These are examples of the self-glorification the ego loves, and they only provide an empty reward, which is unlikely to echo in the hearts of generations to come.

When we begin to heal and move past everything that has left us feeling unfulfilled, empty, and ashamed, and all the things that have held us back from accessing our higher self, we can begin to create our legacy with open-mindedness and intention. Imagine you were able to go back in time and speak to your younger self. What would you say? For me, I'd tell my high-school self that designer clothes don't matter and it's okay that I had acne and braces. I'd help him learn that kindness, integrity, and honesty trump all other qualities. I'd teach my younger self that I don't need to be defined by the trauma or pain I experienced. I'd teach him how to set healthy boundaries, create healthy habits, and learn to tune in to his higher self. Consider for a moment what you would tell your younger self. This is your legacy.

There are souls coming into the world who need the lessons that only you have learned. There are stories only you can tell and secrets that can only be known through the deep vulnerability and honesty of your story. In the 12-step programs, the twelfth step is about sharing with others that which you have learned. That is what legacy is really about. Set an intention to consciously create a legacy that reflects your goals, values, and passions as you see them today. Everything you've ever gone through exists in the collective consciousness and others will go through the same things in their own way.

Writing is one of the best ways to share our lessons and experiences with others and future generations. I love to read the journals of my ancestors who lived in the mid-1800s. Reading about their experiences and trials helps me understand the generational legacy I come from, and in my own dark nights, I've been inspired by the hope and faith that carried my ancestors through theirs.

The journal entries you've been keeping throughout this book and the exercises you've done are a great starting point, but give yourself a chance to share liberally and with vulnerable honesty the things you've gone through and overcome. Imagine thousands of angels, future children, being able to read and benefit from your words. You may not be able to go back in time and teach your younger self the things that could have prevented some of your greatest pain and difficulties, but you can offer that same gift to the people of the future.

Welcome Expansion

Anyone who tries to tell you that the path of spiritual development is always filled with ecstatic bliss is lying or hasn't gone very deep. Spiritual expansion can feel messy, scary, nerve-racking, and uncomfortable. Growing pains are completely normal, and the best thing we can do is welcome them with open arms. Your breath is your best friend. Breathe deeply and sigh it out. The challenges you go through are the raw energy that will be alchemized into the wisdom and power of maturity.

The spiritual expansion process can take us out of our element and force us to confront some uncomfortable aspects of our personalities. Look at it as a detox. You want to release and clear out anything that doesn't serve your highest good. The emotional, psychological, and spiritual detox is necessary and unavoidable. In fact, it actually helps refine and develop our ability to understand and have compassion for the faults and shortcomings of others. As we increase our ability to be patient with ourselves, we can learn to forgive and love those around us with more depth and sincerity.

Some challenges that arise will have their origins in our childhood, or an uncomfortable or traumatic experience. Others will be intergenerational or societal. Some will relate to physical illness or the passing of a loved one. Present moment awareness and tuning in to your observer will help you see these growing pains for what they really are: opportunities for increased understanding and spiritual expansion.

When I opened my first spiritual center, I was introduced to Annelise, a beautiful woman with a contagious smile. She loved to dance, sing, and lead group meditations. I loved her meditations and the unique adventurous spirit she brought to the world. One day, at my Halloween party, she came to me and revealed she had breast cancer. She grabbed a witch's broom and began to dance on the dance floor as if nothing happened.

As she began treatment and her health began to wither, she described her grief, sadness, and pain with eloquence and grace and always made the conscious effort to expand, expand, expand. We often prayed together, and she was always bright with positivity and joy, even through the last conversation we had. Eventually, our sweet, wonderful sister Annelise did pass, but not before teaching us all about acceptance, forgiveness, and love. Annelise was so generous and wonderful, and as a community, we could hardly believe that someone so gifted, so healthy, so vibrant would be taken by cancer. She truly was an angel among us, and still is.

As the journey continues, you become a new person almost every day—a bit wiser, more refined, a little more relaxed, stronger, and more compassionate. You'll find that as you continue, the way you see past experiences changes, too. Through consistent commitment to your spiritual development and welcoming spiritual expansion, you naturally begin to develop the ability to reflect on your past, observe the present, and consider the future without judgment.

Expansion brings with it more opportunities to give freely to others, to share what we've learned, and to support and uplift those around us as they walk through their own challenges. As we stay conscious of the legacy we want to leave, we keep our core values foremost in our minds, allowing us to move artfully and gracefully through the discomfort and surprises that expansion has for us.

My friend often says, "Bless the contrast, it's necessary for our expansion," and she's certainly right. The "contrast" she's referring to is the stark difference between what we'd like to happen and what actually happens. We expand by being able to hold more, do more, and understand more. The transformation happens at the *edge*, not in the comfort zone.

Hold Space for Setbacks

Sometimes it seems that just as you've made progress, taking one step forward, something happens that throws you off balance, causing you to take two steps back. I sometimes call that a "spiritual cha-cha." When this happens, don't be hard on yourself. Acknowledge when you revert to old dysfunctional behavioral patterns, breathe, and move on.

One year, after I had been working very hard on promoting my first book, doing a great job staying balanced and committed to my spiritual practice, I was grateful to have booked a headline speaking engagement at a large wellness conference in Mexico. I fasted, prayed, meditated, studied, and planned diligently—I was not going to blow it! My intention was to make the absolute most of this opportunity and do my best. In the days leading up to my flight to Mexico, I began to feel my anxiety build. What if I didn't do a great job? What if I forgot everything I planned? What if I missed my flight? What if I didn't look my best? As the "what ifs" and anxiety built, I came back to my practice: breathing, relaxing, meditating, and using positive affirmations. They brought me back to center.

Meanwhile, my business partner seemed unsupportive of my trip. Another important project we had been working on for months was at a crucial juncture. It felt as though every conversation I had with her was impossible and everything she said and did was to intentionally sabotage my important trip. I had been doing my best not to let it get to me, but the day before the trip, we got into a heated argument. She began to raise her voice, and I remember my inner dialogue: "Wow. Don't react. She's being totally unreasonable." I breathed in. I breathed out. I felt my blood pressure rising. I felt like everything coming out of her mouth was untrue and unfair, but I kept my calm . . . until I didn't. I yelled right back, dropped everything I was holding, stomped out, got into my car, and drove home to get ready for my trip.

I hated the way I reacted to her just as much as I hated the way she was handling the situation. I felt like a total fraud preparing to go speak at a wellness conference. So, I spoke with my mentor. I meditated. I wrote in my journal, and I began to laugh at myself. I had definitely done a "spiritual cha-cha!" After years of taking steps forward, in one moment of anxiety and anger, I had taken a few steps back. I apologized and did everything I could to repair the relationship with my partner. Then, I focused on what I had to do to teach.

Slip-ups and setbacks like this happen, and the most important thing is that we learn from them. We don't want to brush away our feelings of remorse or contrition completely; these are helpful feelings. They lead us to better resonance with our true self and progress in our journey.

Your setbacks may look different from mine, but find your way to make amends and learn everything you can from your mistakes. We're only human and mistakes are bound to happen. Healing is not linear, and you will go through ups and downs, just as I, and every other person who has ever lived or ever will live, will. Hold space for inevitable setbacks. Be gentle with yourself, practice self-love and self-care. Learn what it means to maintain healthy boundaries and stay true to your passions and purpose.

CARRY THIS WITH YOU

There is a time and season for everything in life. But even as life changes, you can carry your newfound spiritual practice and healing journey into your life beyond this book, through anything that life may present. Things that you find extremely powerful and meaningful today may, one day, become second nature, and you will be able to deepen your practice. Other things that seemed to be helpful may need a refresher. Don't be afraid to customize and alter your practice as time goes on. Although consistency is key, depth is king—meaning, yes, you certainly should make an effort to stay diligent and regular with your practice, but don't let it become rote or shallow. Stick with the basics and allow your understanding of them to deepen over time.

There are three essential aspects of a *Modern Spirituality* practice that will help you take your journey to the next phase. They include:

1. Creating a **formal** spiritual practice for yourself, preferably daily.

2. Incorporating **informal** exercises into your everyday life.

3. Establishing or connecting to a **community** with whom you connect weekly or monthly.

In this context, a "formal" exercise refers to the practices you set aside time for, like meditation, prayer, or a ritual that helps you remember what you've learned and what your goals and values are. This is highly customizable, and everyone will be drawn to something different. One important thing to consider is that the more seriously you take the formal exercises, the more powerfully you will experience their results. This could be as simple as a 20-minute meditation or as elaborate as a combined practice of meditation, journaling, yoga, and study each day. Whatever it is, the commitment and consistency will matter and you can adapt it over time as seasons of your life change.

An informal exercise is about integrating the principles of mindfulness, tuning in to your higher self, and observing the laws of consecration and attraction in everyday life. Infuse your commute with consciousness by being extra mindful of other drivers or passengers around you, of your emotions and energy while you drive, and of the vibration of the music or other content you absorb while traveling. Make meals an informal exercise by taking a moment to express real gratitude for them before you begin to eat, by creating a mealtime ritual and eating mindfully. Incorporate higher consciousness into your self-care routine by being very present as you shower, brush your teeth, and perform other personal care practices. Bring divine order into your home by mindfully completing chores around the house, keeping things tidy, and expressing gratitude for all you have.

The third key component to carrying this spiritual practice into your life is to link up with a community. Not every community will be right for you, and that's okay. You could even consider bringing together two or more friends for a weekly meditation circle, a book club, or a prayer group. Make friends who are also open and committed to spiritual development. Read, study, and set goals together. Celebrate with one another through triumphs and grieve together through heartbreak and loss, always reminding one another of the spiritual principles you stand behind. Don't be afraid to pray and meditate together. We don't have to believe in the same things to pray together, we just have to believe in each other. It takes time to build trust within a community, but it is worth the effort.

Carry with you the beginner's mind, always seeking and finding new wonder and beauty in the world around you. Protect yourself from the ego's trap of being an "expert" and, therefore, able to take shortcuts. The ego will like to say, "Oh, we can skip meditation. I don't need it," or use spiritual jargon to justify overstepping our boundaries. When it comes to spirituality, we are all always beginners. We certainly may be one or two steps ahead of others, but the journey is one of thousands of steps, and the progress to be made is never-ending. Some days, the journey will feel like it is flying by, and on others it will feel like it is dragging on, and really, these are both true. Our lifetimes are but a twinkle in the cosmic memory, but the depth and truth of our lives are rich with meaning. Be brave and be hopeful. You have great powers that will be unlocked as you move forward with faith. Even in the darkest, most painful, tragic moments, remember you are never alone, and that even those moments are working for your growth and benefit. Walk in the light and shine your light in all directions around you. Don't be afraid to be vulnerable, to be honest, and to be seen. Your truth is more beautiful than any lie that even the greatest poet could tell.

THE MODERN SPIRITUAL LIFESTYLE

Consider the three aspects of Modern Spirituality: formal exercise, informal practice, and community. This exercise is designed to support you as you integrate what you've learned in this book and create habits of spiritual living through consciously applying these three aspects.

FORMAL EXERCISES

1. Consider the different formal exercises you experienced in these chapters and in the sidebars.

2. Choose a few small components, like meditation, prayer, and journaling, and bring them together to create a daily ritual. Set a timer for each and choose what kind of meditation you'll commit to.

3. Set yourself up for success by setting alarms on your phone as reminders and planning your schedule around your formal spiritual exercise. Don't worry; you can always adapt your plan and you should change it periodically. The most important element is a consistent formal exercise to keep you centered in your spiritual development process.

INFORMAL PRACTICES

1. Write in your journal about the things you do on any given normal day and consider ways you can turn them into a meditation: meals, personal care, driving, commuting, walking—anything can be done mindfully and, therefore, become an informal practice.

2. Meditate and visualize yourself doing these things mindfully, where you normally do them, and imagine the nuanced differences in how you will now try to do them in your life.

3. Go easy on yourself. This journey is about transitioning into a completely new way of being. You won't get it right all the time. Aim for progress, not perfection.

COMMUNITY

1. In your journal, make a list of friends and family members whom you may consider part of your spiritual community.

2. Write a list of exercises or activities you may like to do with them. This could be prayer and meditation groups, a book club, or a Modern Spirituality group. Get creative and don't stress over it.

3. Make a plan. Pick one activity and invite friends to join you. Don't worry if some decline, and don't take it personally. Celebrate and embrace anyone who will join you, even if it's just one friend. Let it be fun and make it your own.

RESOURCES

The Ancient Wisdom by Annie Besant

Daily Mindfulness: 365 Exercises to Deepen Your Practice and Find Peace by Benjamin W. Decker

Everyday Amenti: A Guided Journey for Cultivating a Feather-Light Heart by Jennifer Sodini

The Initiates of the Flame by Manly P. Hall

Initiation, Human and Solar by Alice A. Bailey

Meditations on Christ: A 5-Minute Guided Journal for Christians by Benjamin W. Decker

Nature by Ralph Waldo Emerson

A New Earth: Awakening to Your Life's Purpose by Eckhart Tolle

Practical Meditation for Beginners: 10 Days to a Happier, Calmer You by Benjamin W. Decker

The Religion of Tomorrow by Ken Wilber

A Return to Love by Marianne Williamson

The Secret Doctrine by Helena Blavatsky

The Secret Teachings of All Ages by Manly P. Hall

Spiritual Liberation: Fulfilling Your Soul's Potential by Michael Beckwith

INDEX

ACKNOWLEDGMENTS

Honor and respect go to my lineage of ancestors and spiritual teachers who have been with me throughout the process of writing this work, and in loving memory of Ellie, Tom, June, Philip, and Barbara.

Thank you to my parents, Jeff and Karma Decker, who diligently maintained connection to the faith, and to my brothers Andrew, Chris, Chad, and Scott, and their perfect families for doing the same.

Love and thanks to Marianne Williamson, who held my hand through great pain, opened my heart, brought me to reconciliation with my childhood religion, held me to high standards, and lives a powerful example of spirituality in action.

Gratitude and love to Dr. Ronald Alexander for his friendship and honesty, to Jennifer Sodini for her knowledge and insight, to Kristin Lagan for her trust and generosity, to Ansley Weller for her faith and wisdom, to Nancy and James Odom for their patience and support, to Felicia Tomasko for seeing me in my individuality, to AnnaLynne McCord for understanding me, to Sharon Salzberg for inspiring me, and to Jeff Kraso, Suze Yalof Schwartz, Elaine Duncan, Tal Rabinowitz, Jeffrey Segal, Dmitriy Khanzhin, Darcie Odom, Bianka Kureti, Shannon Algeo, Chelsea Comfort, Atlas Blake, Jacob Hanson, Caitlin Crosby, Cassandra Bodzak, Megan Monahan, Camilla Sacre-Dallerup, Matthew Coelho, Christopher Gialanella, Jorge Perez, Chris Pan, Lauren Selsky, Tandra Steiner, Wendy Zahler, Lisa Hall, Tarah Bird, Alexandra De Martini, Orion Solarion, Laurasia Mattingly, Jordana Reim, Andrew Keegan, Susan Stanger, Julia Nugent, Mia Banducci, Light Watkins, Jessie May Wolfe, Frank Elaridi, Bryant Wood, Jeannette Ceja, Claire Clark, Rosie Acosta, Sahara Rose, Lauren Von Der Pool, Arezu Kaywanfar, Susy Schieffelin, Amanda Gilbert, Jessica Hall, Katie Cleary, Be Solomon, Mary Cassells, and Rachel Fox for believing in me. Great love and honor go to those many other names who have not been mentioned here.

ABOUT THE AUTHOR

Benjamin W. Decker is a world-renowned meditation teacher, anti–human trafficking activist, and passionate public speaker on topics of spirituality, wellness, and peacemaking. He was born in Durango, Colorado, to descendants of the founding pioneer families of The Church of Jesus Christ of Latter-day Saints and is a graduate of the Church's seminary program. Decker is the co-founder of the Fireside Library of World Religion, Politics, and Philosophy. He was also the founding Partnerships Director for the anti–human trafficking organization Unlikely Heroes and is the former Partnerships Director for the humanitarian organization Generosity.org, a founding meditation teacher at The DEN Meditation and Unplug Meditation, and founding spiritual director of Full Circle Venice.